# Eyewitness
# Mummy

Arrowheads from Egyptian sand grave, around 3000 BCE

Slate palette from Egyptian grave, around 3000 BCE

Gold ear spools from ancient Peruvian grave

Chancay pottery figure from a Peruvian burial

Peruvian doll buried with mummy

Case for mummy of shrew mouse, Egyptian, around 600 BCE

Ancient Egyptian canopic jars, to hold internal organs of sacred Apis Bull (left) and person (right)

Peruvian pot from grave

Wooden figure of Anubis, the ancient Egyptian god of embalming

# Eyewitness
# Mummy

Hand from ancient Egyptian mummy with individually wrapped fingers

Written by
## JAMES PUTNAM

Photographed by
## PETER HAYMAN

Wooden face from ancient Egyptian mummy case

Magical amulets with heads of four Sons of Horus

**DK**
DK Publishing

Wedjat eye amulet

Flint knife found in ancient Egyptian grave, around 3000 BCE

Faience (glazed) hand

Head from Egyptian mummy

LONDON, NEW YORK,
MELBOURNE, MUNICH, AND DELHI

**Project editor** Scott Steedman
**Art editor** Bob Gordon
**Managing editor** Helen Parker
**Managing art editor** Julia Harris
**Production** Louise Barratt
**Picture research** Cynthia Hole
**Editorial consultants** The Department of Egyptian
Antiquities, British Museum

### Revised Editions

**Editorial** Kitty Blount, Sue Malyan, Jayne Miller
**Design** Rebecca Johns, Edward Kinsey
**Managing editor** Camilla Hallinan
**Managing art editors** Jane Thomas, Owen Peyton Jones
**Art director** Martin Wilson
**Associate publisher** Andrew Macintyre
**Production editors** Jenny Jacoby, Laragh Kedwell
**Production controllers** Jen Lockwood, Pip Tinsley
**Picture research** Sarah Pownall, Myriam Megharbi
**U.S. editorial** Elizabeth Hester, Beth Sutinis
**U.S. design and DTP** Dirk Kaufman, Milos Orlovic
**U.S. production** Chris Avgherinos

This Eyewitness ® Guide has been conceived by
Dorling Kindersley Limited and Editions Gallimard

First published in the United States in 1993
This revised edition published in 2004, 2009 by DK Publishing,
375 Hudson Street, New York, New York, 10014

A catalog record for this book is available from
the Library of Congress.
ISBN 978-0-7566-4541-0 (HC); 978-0-7566-0706-7 (ALB)

Color reproduction by Colourscan, Singapore
Printed by Toppan Co., (Shenzhen) Ltd., China

Discover more at
**www.dk.com**

Chimu
mummy
bundle

Gilded wooden
coffin of ancient
Egyptian priestess,
around 1250 BCE

# Contents

Egyptian pot containing linen mummy bandages, around 2000 BCE

# What are mummies?

MUMMIES ARE THE PRESERVED BODIES of people or animals. The word was first used to describe the bandaged bodies of ancient Egyptians. But any dead body that still has skin on it is a mummy. If people die or are buried in the right conditions, they may be mummified (preserved) by accident (pp. 8–9). This can happen in wet, marshy places (pp. 58–59), or in the freezing cold of mountains or the polar regions. But most often, people are preserved by being dried out. Many cultures have developed a chemical process—called embalming—to achieve this artificially. The ancient Egyptians are famous for their skillful embalming and their elaborate burial customs. But people all over the world have embalmed their dead. Wherever it is practiced, mummification is usually done for religious reasons. Most cultures believe in some kind of afterlife (life after death). By preserving a dead person's body in recognizable form, they hope to prepare him or her for a better future life.

**STUFFED ANIMALS**
Unlike mummies, stuffed animals are usually little more than dried skin complete with feathers or fur. The taxidermist props this up with a wire framework to make a lifelike animal.

**WHY MUMMY?**
Egyptian mummies were coated in dark resins. The Arabs (who invaded Egypt in the seventh century CE) thought this was bitumen, and called them *mummiya*, the Arabic word for bitumen.

**OUR LEADER**
Famous people are sometimes mummified. The Russian revolutionary leader Vladimir Lenin was preserved using a secret technique that involved paraffin wax. Millions of people have traveled to Moscow to see his body lying in state in Red Square.

**ALL WRAPPED UP**
This is one of the earliest ancient Egyptian mummies, from 2400 BCE. Egyptian mummies are often carefully wrapped in hundreds of yards of linen bandages (pp. 16–17).

**INTO THE AFTERLIFE**
The Egyptians believed that a person's soul left the body at death (pp. 12–13). After the burial, the soul was reunited with the body, and the mummy lived on in the afterlife. For all this to happen, the body had to be well preserved. Then it was bandaged and laid in a coffin or mummy case. The technique of embalming developed gradually over ancient Egypt's long history. It reached its peak around 1000 BCE, but Romans living in Egypt were still being mummified in the third century CE pp. 42–43). This well-wrapped mummy of a 50-year-old man probably dates from 900 to 750 BCE.

*False beard*

*Mummy wrapped in linen bandages*

*Base of mummy case*

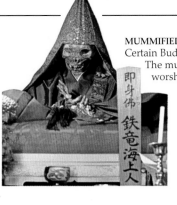

## MUMMIFIED BUDDHA
Certain Buddhist priests in Japan had a tradition of mummification. The mummies were set up in temples, where they were worshiped like statues. The priests who became mummies were given the title *Sokushin-butsu*, which means "a Buddha of the body." This is the priest Tetsuryukai. He participated in his own mummification by eating a special grain-free diet for the three years before he died, in 1868. Then the other priests smoke-dried his body with huge candles.

*Hooded parka made of sealskin*

## NICE HAIR
This skull from a female Egyptian mummy dates from around 1600 BCE. As sometimes happens, the flesh has decayed but the tougher hair has been preserved.

## STOPPING THE ROT
Ancient Egyptian embalmers realized that a body's internal organs were the first to decay. So they removed the lungs, liver, stomach, and intestines through an incision in the left side (pp. 14–15). The brain was usually extracted through the nose. The empty body could then be dried out by covering it in natron, a naturally occurring salt. Embalm literally means "in balsam," a sweet-smelling oil. After they had been dried, Egyptian mummies were coated in ointments, oils, and resins, to keep the skin supple and lifelike.

## THE MUMMY'S HOUSE
Egyptian mummies were usually buried in tombs. In the Old Kingdom (2686–2181 BCE), the pharaohs (Egyptian kings) built pyramid tombs. These are the famous pyramids at Giza. The largest of the three, the Great Pyramid of Khufu, was made of 2,300,000 blocks of stone and stood 487 ft (146 m) high. Because the mummies were buried inside with many treasures, the pyramids were robbed in ancient times.

*Mummy case lid*

*Painted figures of gods*

## BABY MUMMY
This six-month-old Inuit boy died around 1475. He is one of eight well-preserved mummies discovered on a jagged cliff in Greenland in 1972. Following Inuit tradition, he had been dressed in warm clothes and left with objects to help him in the next world. Protected from the sun and snow by a rocky overhang, the boy's body was slowly freeze-dried by the cold Arctic air (p. 63).

## GOLDEN PHARAOH
Probably the best known pharaoh is Tutankhamun (pp. 38–39). He was not an important ruler, but his intact tomb, found in 1922, was crammed with treasures and beautiful works of art. This is his mummy mask, made of solid gold. Compared to many pharaohs, his mummy was in poor condition.

# Natural mummies

SOME OF THE MOST REMARKABLE MUMMIES have been preserved by accident. Natural mummies are usually found in extreme climates where dry sands or freezing cold have somehow stopped the process of decay. Decay is caused by bacteria, which breed in the water that makes up over 70 percent of a person's body weight. Hot desert sands can preserve a body by dehydrating it (drying it out). Bodies buried in the icy polar regions may be so thoroughly frozen that decay never starts. Occasionally, bodies have been freeze-dried by a combination of cold temperatures and very dry winds, as found in some mountain caves (pp. 7, 63). In northern Europe, the unusual conditions found in marshy bogs have also preserved bodies remarkably well.

Flint knife buried in sand with body

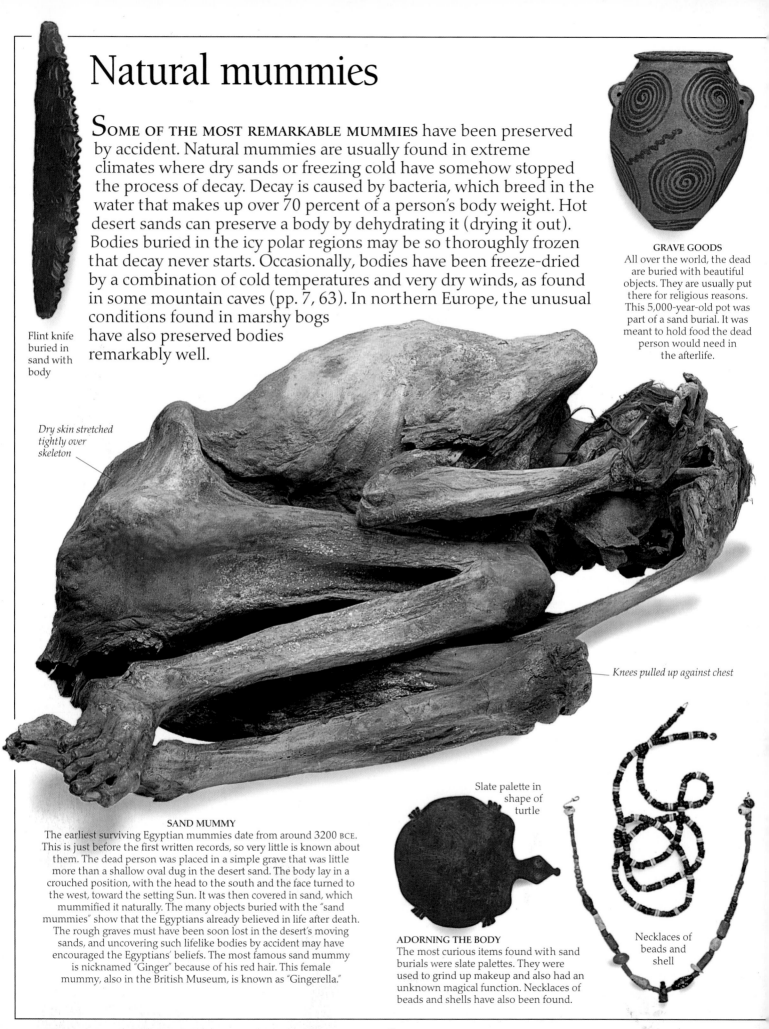

**GRAVE GOODS**
All over the world, the dead are buried with beautiful objects. They are usually put there for religious reasons. This 5,000-year-old pot was part of a sand burial. It was meant to hold food the dead person would need in the afterlife.

Dry skin stretched tightly over skeleton

Knees pulled up against chest

Slate palette in shape of turtle

**SAND MUMMY**
The earliest surviving Egyptian mummies date from around 3200 BCE. This is just before the first written records, so very little is known about them. The dead person was placed in a simple grave that was little more than a shallow oval dug in the desert sand. The body lay in a crouched position, with the head to the south and the face turned to the west, toward the setting Sun. It was then covered in sand, which mummified it naturally. The many objects buried with the "sand mummies" show that the Egyptians already believed in life after death. The rough graves must have been soon lost in the desert's moving sands, and uncovering such lifelike bodies by accident may have encouraged the Egyptians' beliefs. The most famous sand mummy is nicknamed "Ginger" because of his red hair. This female mummy, also in the British Museum, is known as "Gingerella."

**ADORNING THE BODY**
The most curious items found with sand burials were slate palettes. They were used to grind up makeup and also had an unknown magical function. Necklaces of beads and shells have also been found.

Necklaces of beads and shell

## BODY CAST

Over 2,000 ancient Romans died in 79 CE when the town of Pompeii was engulfed by a huge eruption of Mount Vesuvius. The volcanic ash set around their bodies like wet cement. Over the years, the bodies decayed, and the ash turned to solid rock. A perfect mold of the body shape survived. When the ruins of Pompeii were excavated, these body hollows were discovered and a method of filling them with liquid plaster was developed. This created a perfect replica of the dead person, like a mummy with flesh of plaster.

*Trace of clothing wrapped around body*

## TOLLUND MAN

This is the head of a man discovered in the Tollund Bog in Denmark in 1950. He has been dead for more than 2,000 years, but looks like he is just sleeping. He was found with a noose around his neck and is thought to have been sacrificed and thrown into the bog as part of a spring fertility ritual (pp. 58–59).

*Noose*

*Stubble, thought to be two or three days' growth*

*Sheepskin cap tied under the chin*

### ICY GRAVE

This is John Torrington, one of three well-preserved mummies discovered by scientists in the Canadian Arctic in 1984. They were English sailors who had died on Sir John Franklin's tragic expedition to find the Northwest Passage. Franklin left England with two ships in 1845 and was never seen again. "It's as if he's just unconscious" marveled one of the scientists as he lifted Torrington from his icy coffin.

### BUILDER'S SACRIFICE

Mummies of animals are sometimes found in ordinary houses. Cold drafts of air may freeze-dry the bodies of mice that die in walls or under floorboards. In 16th- and 17th-century England, builders used to place a dead animal in a nook somewhere and board it up with a few lucky items. This is a mummified chicken, found behind a brick wall in a 17th-century house in London.

# A land lost in time

THE ANCIENT EGYPTIANS went to great lengths to preserve their bodies and their worldly possessions. This has helped the world to rediscover ancient Egypt. The civilization of the pharaohs flourished by the Nile River for over 3,000 years. But until the French invaded Egypt in 1798, it had been virtually forgotten. The travelers who visited the country were amazed by its ancient monuments and tombs covered in mysterious hieroglyphics (picture-writing). People have been reopening tombs in search of treasures since ancient times. But until recently, they paid little attention to the mummies. We now know that with the help of modern science, these timeless bodies can tell us amazing things about life and death in the ancient land.

**LANDS OF THE NILE**
Egypt is mostly desert, and life has always been concentrated along the banks of the Nile River. In ancient times, the land was often divided in two. The northern part, which included the fertile Nile delta, was called Lower Egypt. In the south was Upper Egypt, which included a large area now flooded by the huge Aswan Dam.

**OLD KING'S TOMB**
The period we call ancient Egypt began around 3000 BCE. The step pyramid at Saqqara was built around 2650 BCE, in the Old Kingdom. This was followed by the Middle and New Kingdoms, the Late Period, and then an era when Egypt was ruled by the Greeks and later the Romans.

**TOMB GUARD**
Beautiful statues were placed in tombs for religious reasons. This painted wooden statue represents the god Anubis. He has the head of a jackal or wild dog. Anubis was the ancient god of the dead, associated with mummification and guardian of the cemeteries.

**NEST FOR A MUMMY**
After it was embalmed and wrapped, the mummy was laid in a coffin. This might be the first in a whole series (or nest) of mummy cases. The Egyptians believed these cases would magically protect the body. They were covered in elaborate paintings and spells to help the mummy's spirit on its difficult path through the afterlife.

**FAMILIAR FACE?**
The ancient Egyptians took extra care preserving the features of the face. This was because they believed the dead person's spirit had to return to the tomb and recognize its body before the mummy could live forever (pp. 12–13).

*Texture of tight linen bandages impressed on skin*

**NAPOLEON MEETS A MUMMY**
The French were the first Europeans to study ancient Egypt seriously. When Napoleon Bonaparte invaded Egypt in 1798, he brought a team of scholars and artists with him. Napoleon was fascinated by the ancient land and collected several mummies himself.

## ANCIENT LIVES

The ancient Egyptians decorated the walls of tombs with beautiful paintings that tell us a lot about their everyday lives. Paintings that show people farming, hunting, feasting, relaxing, and attending religious and royal ceremonies have all been found.

## MUMMY TRADE

Excavating in Egypt's hot, dusty climate is tiring. This is a dig in the 1900s. By then, mummies could be sold for a high price. In the 16th and 17th centuries, they were ground up and used in medicines. Local people also used them as fuel—they are soaked in resins so burn well.

*Idealized image of dead person*

*Wig*

*Elaborate collar*

*Beetle god holding Sun*

## FATHER OF EGYPTOLOGY

It took the French scholar Jean-François Champollion (1790–1832) most of his life to decipher hieroglyphics, the ancient Egyptian picture-writing. He announced his first breakthrough in 1822. This allowed Egyptologists to read the inscriptions that were all over statues, tombs, temples, and mummy cases.

Illustration from the opening page of *The Description of Egypt*, published from 1809 to 1822 by the team of scholars that went with Napoleon.

## TIME CAPSULE

Inside the wrappings of this mummy is a middle-aged Roman man. X-rays show that he suffered from arthritis of the spine (pp. 48–51).

*Winged gods*

*Ankh, symbol of life*

*Spell for dead person's soul written in hieroglyphics*

## STRANGE SYMBOLS

Mummy cases are covered in religious symbols meant to help the dead person. Only when they could read hieroglyphics could Egyptologists begin to make sense of the Egyptians' complex religious beliefs. The writings often give the name and title of the dead person, and sometimes his or her father or mother too.

# The Egyptian Book of the Dead

Iᴛ's ᴄᴀʟʟᴇᴅ ᴀ ʙᴏᴏᴋ, but the Egyptian Book of the Dead is really a collection of magic spells. By about 1400 ʙᴄᴇ, they were usually written on a roll of papyrus, the Egyptians' form of paper. There were over 200 spells, which the Egyptians called "The Spells for Coming Forth by Day." Each spell was a prayer or a plea from the dead person and was meant to help on the difficult voyage to the next world. The ancient Egyptians believed every person had several spirit forms, the most important being the *Ka* and the *Ba*. The *Ka* was the vital energy of life. Like any living thing, the *Ka* needed food and drink, which the Egyptians provided through offerings or images of food placed in the tomb (p. 31). A person's character and ability to move around was called its *Ba*. The *Ba* is something like our idea of a person's spirit or soul and was usually pictured as a bird. For a person to live forever, his or her *Ba* and *Ka* had to be reunited in the tomb with the mummy. Once this happened, the mummy became an immortal (or *Akh*).

**HARD-WORKING SPELL**
Shabti figures (pp. 32–33) are painted with a spell promising they will work for the dead person in the afterlife.

**GOLD HEART**
This gold heart scarab is an amulet (pp. 20–21) worn by the mummy for protection. It is inscribed with a spell to help the heart when it was weighed (p. 13). An ancient papyrus records that robbers brought to trial in 1125 ʙᴄᴇ confessed that they had stolen it from the tomb of Pharaoh Sobkemsaf II.

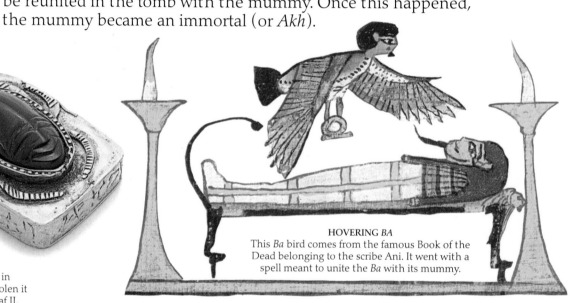

**HOVERING BA**
This *Ba* bird comes from the famous Book of the Dead belonging to the scribe Ani. It went with a spell meant to unite the *Ba* with its mummy.

**FIRST BOOKS**
In the Old Kingdom, over 4,000 years ago, magic spells were inscribed on the inner walls of pyramids. By the Middle Kingdom, they were painted inside coffins, like this one from 2000 ʙᴄᴇ. The first Book of the Dead on papyrus dates from around 1400 ʙᴄᴇ.

**RISE, MUMMY!**
*Ba* birds have human heads. This little statue was probably originally attached to the foot of a mummy case. The *Ba* is raising its arms, as if it is telling the mummy's spirit to rise. Two outstretched human arms were the hieroglyphic symbol for the *Ka*.

Set of tools used in the
Opening of the Mouth

*Forked tool used to touch
mummy's face*

*Adze, a
tool held up to
mummy's face*

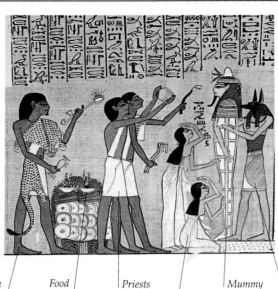

### OPEN UP
During the funeral, the
mummy went through
an important ritual
called the Opening of
the Mouth. The ancient
Egyptians believed this
would restore the mummy's
senses, so it could eat, drink,
and enjoy the afterlife
properly. This illustration
is from the Book of the
Dead by the scribe Hunefer,
from around 1310 BCE.

*Priest in leopard skin
burning incense*

*Food
offerings*

*Priests*

*Mummy*

*Mourners*

*Priest wearing Anubis mask*

### JACKAL HEAD
This Anubis mask has a
moving jaw. It may have
been worn by a priest
during rituals like the
Opening of the Mouth.

*Jury of gods sits
in judgment*

### WEIGHING THE HEART
The most important
moment in a mummy's
"life" was the weighing
of its heart. In this
ceremony, a jury of gods
decided whether the
mummy had behaved
well enough on Earth
to deserve eternal life.
This was calculated by
weighing the mummy's
heart against a feather,
the symbol of truth.
The jackal god Anubis
performed the ceremony,
and Thoth, the scribe
god, took notes. If sins
on Earth had made the
mummy's heart too
heavy, it was thrown
to the monster Ammit,
who devoured it. But if
the heart balanced with
the Feather of Truth, the
mummy had passed
the test and would
live forever.

*Dead man watches
anxiously with wife*

*Ba bird*

*Heart*

*Anubis, the jackal
god, keeps eye on scales*

*Feather of Truth*

*Thoth, the scribe god,
writes down result*

*Monster Ammit with crocodile's
head waits to devour heart*

### BOOK HOLDER
This wooden statue of Osiris, the god
of rebirth (pp. 34–35), was placed in
a tomb. It has a secret compartment
where the Book of the Dead
was hidden.

*Roll of
papyrus*

*Base*

*Secret
compartment*

### EGYPTIAN PAPER
The scribes, ancient
Egypt's full-time
writers, usually copied
the Book of the Dead
onto papyrus. This reed
grows in marshes by the
Nile. Strips of papyrus
were woven together
and beaten to form
long rolls like paper.

# Making a mummy

Wooden jackal, representing Anubis, the god of embalming

"MY CORPSE IS PERMANENT, it will not perish nor be destroyed in this land forever." So ends spell 154 in the Book of the Dead (pp. 12–13). From the earliest sand burials 5,000 years ago (p. 8), the Egyptians could see that a body had to be dried to stop it from rotting away. They developed a method of drying with natron, a natural salt that left a corpse more flexible and lifelike than drying with hot sand. Natron absorbs water. It also dissolves body fats and is a mild antiseptic that kills destructive bacteria. Embalming traditionally took 70 days, of which 40 were taken up drying the body. But first of all the vital organs, which decay the fastest, had to be removed. Only the heart, which the mummy would need when it was judged in the next world (p. 13), was left. The body was then washed with palm wine and spices and covered in natron. Later, molten (liquid) resin, taken from trees, was poured over the body to help preserve it. To stop it from cracking, the skin was rubbed with a mixture of cedar oil, wax, natron, and gum. Then the body was packed with wads of linen, sand, or even sawdust, to give it shape. Finally, the mummy was ready to be wrapped in layers of linen bandages.

**EMBALMING EYEWITNESS**
The Greek historian Herodotus visited Egypt in 450 BCE and wrote the only eyewitness account of embalming. "In the best treatment" he observed, "first of all they draw out the brains through the nostrils with an iron hook… Next they make an incision in the flank with a sharp obsidian blade through which they can extract all the internal organs. Then they clean out the body cavity, rinsing it with palm wine…(then) they cover the corpse with natron for seventy days, but for no longer, and so mummify it. After the seventy days are up they wash the corpse and wrap it from head to toe in bandages of the finest linen anointed with gum."

**FOUR DUMMIES**
The mummy's internal organs were embalmed separately. By about 2000 BCE, they were then placed in containers called canopic jars. These little coffins had heads, either of gods or the dead person. By 1000 BCE, the wrapped organs were put back in the mummy. But dummy canopic jars with nothing in them were still put in the tomb. These dummy jars have the heads of the four gods known as the sons of Horus (p. 20).

Imsety, with a person's head, guarded the liver

Qebehsenuef, a falcon, held the intestines

Hapy, a baboon, kept an eye on the lungs

Duamutef, a jackal, guarded the stomach

*Body* / *Embalmers pour water from jugs* / Body, black from oils and resins, is purified with streams of water

*Embalmers* / *Head embalmer wearing Anubis mask* / Lying on bier (couch), body is covered in dry crystals of natron

### CANOPIC CHEST
This wooden chest belonged to a doctor named Gua, who died around 2050 BCE. It contains his four canopic jars. They have human heads—it wasn't until 1500 BCE that the sons of Horus became common as stoppers.

*Wooden stoppers*

*Jars made of the rock calcite*

### BRAIN HOOKS
A rod was usually pushed up the nose to punch a hole into the skull. Then bronze hooks or spoons could be poked in to scoop out the brain.

*Head support*

*Embalming incision*

*Wax embalming plate with wedjat eye decoration*

### BOWL OF NATRON
A natural salt, natron was found around the edges of desert lakes near Cairo.

*Ritual knife with gold handle and flint blade*

### EMBALMING TOOLS
The embalming incision was usually made on the left side of the body. Herodotus says the knife blade was made of obsidian, a kind of volcanic glass that had to be imported from Ethiopia. But all the ritual knives that have been found have blades of flint. After the organs had been removed, the incision was covered by a plate decorated with a wedjat eye (p. 20).

### WHERE THE SUN SETS...
Cemeteries, tombs, and embalmers' workshops were usually on the west bank of the Nile. The Egyptians believed this desert area where the Sun set every evening was the land of the dead.

### STEP BY STEP
The best pictures of embalming are painted on the mummy case of Djedbastiufankh, from about 600 BCE. This case is now in the Hildesheim Museum, Germany.

*Wrapped mummy*

*Canopic jar*

Mummy, bandaged and wearing a mask (pp. 18–19), is attended by Anubis

### WELL PRESERVED
Considering that she was mummified after 600 BCE, around the time Herodotus visited Egypt, this woman has been remarkably well embalmed. By then, the empire was collapsing and the art of embalming was in decline. Embalmers still made sure the mummy looked good on the outside, but they didn't bother much with the insides. Usually bodies were simply coated from head to toe in resin.

# Wrapping up

**NEED A HAND?**
Each finger on this 3,000-year-old mummified hand has been individually wrapped. It is wearing a gold ring set with a scarab beetle (p. 44). Rings and other jewelry were often specially made just to be worn by mummies.

*Gold ring*

**THE FINAL SHROUD**
The wrapping was completed by a shroud. This covered the entire mummy and was held in place by a long bandage running from head to toe and crossed by horizontal bands.

HUNDREDS OF YARDS OF LINEN went into the careful wrapping of a mummy. The linen didn't just come in the well-known rolls of bandages. Mummies were also wrapped in shrouds, large sheets of material that were thrown over the body like a cape. Each shroud had to be long enough to be knotted at the top, behind the mummy's head, and down below under the feet. As many as 20 alternating layers of bandages and shrouds have been counted on one mummy. The exact arrangement of the rolls and shrouds of linen varied a lot from period to period and can be helpful in dating mummies. The first layer was usually a shroud. Then each finger and toe was wrapped up separately. Next, a long strip of linen beginning at the right shoulder was crisscrossed over the head. To hold the head up, a strap was then passed under the chin and knotted on top of the head. As more bandages were added, they were kept very tight to maintain the mummy's distinctive shape. Protective amulets (pp. 20–21) and sometimes the dead person's jewelry were placed between the layers. At the same time, the linen was constantly brushed with sticky, liquid resin. This glued the bandages together and made them slowly stiffen as they dried. Around 15 days were set aside for the wrapping, and the whole process was accompanied by much prayer and ritual.

*Inscription in hieroglyphic*

**SHROUD FRAGMENT**
Numbers had many meanings to the ancient Egyptians. Traditionally, mummies were wrapped in seven shrouds, since this was a magical number. The outer shroud was often painted with magical writings and spells to protect the mummy within.

**IT'S A WRAP**
In this imaginative picture of a wrapping, an assistant is busy pouring the resin used to hold the bandages together. Lying on a special bier (couch), the mummy is being wrapped in stages, supervised by the chief embalmer. Priests kneel at the feet of the mummy, reciting sacred spells. In the background, more assistants are trying to get the mummy case (pp. 22–27) down the stairs.

**OVERSEEING THE MYSTERIES**
A special embalmer called the Overseer of Mysteries chose the pieces of linen to go on the head. The eye sockets were covered by pads of linen, and strips were plastered over the face.

*Jaw bone*

*Hair*

**HAIR MAGIC**
A lost hair could be used against the mummy if it fell into enemy hands. So the dead person's hair was gathered together and laid in the tomb with the mummy.

Final
shroud

Writing used
to date linen

**LINEN OF YESTERDAY**
All the wrappings above were unrolled from the
same mummy. The linen varies a lot in quality. The
cheapest was old household cloth. This explains a sad
Egyptian funeral song in which the dead person is said to
be sleeping in the "cast-off linen of yesterday." This domestic
linen is well worn and has often been darned. The best
mummy wrappings were clothes used to dress statues
of gods in the temples. Writing on wrappings can
be used to date mummies.

A French archeologist
discovers a mummy in the
ruins of Antinoe, 1896

**ROMAN BOY**
Inside these wrappings is the
body of a Roman boy. X-rays
show that he was about eight
when he died. He is lying with his
hands by his sides and is wearing
a bracelet on his right wrist.

**TOOTSIES**
Even the toenails on this
beautifully bandaged foot have
been individually wrapped.

# Mummy masks

A BEAUTIFUL MASK did more than protect the mummy's face—it could also act as a substitute head if the mummy's real head was lost or damaged. When the dead person's spirit (the *Ba*, p. 12) returned to the tomb, it could recognize the mummy by its mask. One of the most famous works of art in the world is the stunning gold mask found on Tutankhamun's mummy (pp. 7, 39). The masks of pharaohs may all have been made of solid gold, often inlaid with beautiful gemstones. The use of gold was connected to the belief that the Sun god, with whom the mummy hoped to be united, had flesh of pure gold. Less important mummies wore masks made from cartonnage, a sort of papier-mâché of linen or scrap papyrus gummed together with plaster or resin. The wet cartonnage was molded to fit the mummy. Once it had hardened, it could then be gilded (covered in gold leaf) or painted in rich colors.

*Floral wreath*

*Gold earrings*

*Bead necklace*

*Winged scarab beetle*

**ALL DRESSED UP AND NOWHERE TO GO**
This Roman mummy mask shows a woman dressed up in her best clothes and wearing her favorite jewelry. She is even wearing makeup so she will look her best for the gods.

*Sacred flower*

*Bracelet*

*Gold headdress with wings of a vulture*

*Striped wig*

**NOBEL MASK**
This cartonnage mask, from about 1500 BCE, is thought to have belonged to a wealthy woman named Satdjehuty. The beautiful vulture headdress she is wearing suggests that she must have been a noblewoman.

*Prayer to Osiris to provide food*

*Prayer to Anubis for a good burial*

*Raised relief coated in gold*

**GREEK GOLD**
Cartonnage mummy masks were particularly popular by Greek and Roman times (pp. 42–43). This elegant gilded mask is rich in raised decoration, a typical feature of the period.

*Floral wreath*

*Curly wig*

### SPITTING IMAGE
Ancient Egyptian masks were usually idealized, with perfect features and a calm and noble expression. Greek mummies (pp. 42–43) wore more personal masks with realistic features and vividly painted details. These masks seem to represent real people.

### WOODEN FEATURES
This mask was carved from wood and then painted. It comes from 1350 BCE—the same period in which Tutankhamun was pharaoh (pp. 38–39).

*Pierced ears for wearing studs*

*Collar of lotus petals*

*Eye of Horus (wedjat eye)*

*Ba (soul) bird*

### EVERY PICTURE TELLS A STORY
This cartonnage mask from the Roman period is gilded and painted with many religious scenes. Glass eyes were added to create a more lifelike appearance.

*Gods holding the Feather of Truth*

*Linen strips holding mask and pectoral in place*

*Pectoral, a painted cartonnage chest decoration*

### TIED DOWN
After the careful embalming and wrapping processes, the mask was finally fitted over the mummy's head. It was then lashed in place with more bandages. Often a decorated pectoral (chest plate) and foot case (p. 27) were added in the same way.

# Amulets and magic charms

Egyptian faience hand placed on a mummy

Two-finger amulet laid on embalming incision

ANCIENT EGYPTIANS WORE AMULETS after they died, just as they did in life. They believed these charms had magical properties to protect the body from evil or bring good luck. Many different kinds of amulet, often representing plants, animals, or parts of the body, were placed among a mummy's wrappings. Several hundred amulets have been found on a single mummy. They were positioned on the body according to the Book of the Dead (pp. 12–13), and many were inscribed with extracts from these sacred writings. The particular stone or material used for the amulet was believed to give it extra power. Priests often spoke spells and prayers as the sacred amulets were placed on the mummy.

**THE THREE GRACES**
Between them, the mother goddess, Isis (right), her son, Horus, (center), and her sister, Nephthys, (left) gave powerful overall protection to the mummy.

**EYE OF HORUS**
According to an ancient legend, the god Horus had his eye miraculously restored after he had lost it in a fight with evil. This eye symbol, known as the wedjat eye, became connected to healing. It was thought to protect the mummy's health and give the body new vitality.

Taweret

Bes

**ODD COUPLE**
The pregnant hippopotamus Taweret was the goddess of childbirth. Her lion-maned assistant, Bes, was a smiling dwarf who protected women and children.

**FOUR SONS OF HORUS**
These amulets guarded the vital organs usually removed and placed in canopic jars (pp. 14–15). They are made from Egyptian faience, a type of glazed ware.

Imsety
(human head)

Duamutef
(jackal head)

Qebehsenuef
(falcon head)

Hapy
(baboon head)

**HEAD WARMER**
This bronze disk was tucked under a mummy's head. It carried a spell meant to keep the head warm.

Headrest amulet made of obsidian

*Plaited wig*

*Real rings*

*Stone ear studs*

*Gilded mask*

*Wooden arms*

Scarab beetle

Holes for sewing into bandages

Beetle's wings, made of faience

**WINGED HEART SCARAB**
Egyptians thought that intelligence dwelled in the heart, not the brain. This heart amulet made sure that the mummy went into the afterlife with all of his or her wits intact.

Falcon head

**STAIRWAY TO HEAVEN**
These steps symbolize the stairs on Osiris' throne, which every mummy's spirit would have to climb (pp. 34–35).

Papyrus reed (p. 13)

Scarab beetle

Girdle of Isis

**GIRDLE OF ISIS**
This knot amulet represents Isis, the mother goddess. It is made of red stone, to represent her blood. Placed on the chest, the girdle was a powerful symbol that protected the mummy.

Head of a lioness

Counterpoise, made of blue faience

Heart, made from a red-and-white stone called breccia

Heart scarab

**CLOSE TO THE MUMMY'S HEART**
This heart scarab has no wings. These important amulets were often set in a frame and sewn on top of the mummy's wrappings. The ancient Egyptians thought that the scarab beetle was born magically from a ball of dung (p. 44). So it was not surprising that they associated it with rebirth after death. A spell from the Book of the Dead that would help in the Weighing of the Heart (p. 13) was written on the other side of the amulet.

Shen, a circle of cord, a symbol of completeness and eternity

Plaque showing Anubis

Shabti figure

**WELL PROTECTED**
The upper part of the body usually received most of the amulets, with many grouped around the heart or just below the waist. This female mummy is protected by a fine selection of amulets. She is also wearing some of her favorite jewelry.

Nut, the sky goddess, wrapping her wings around the mummy

Outer mummy
case base

Inner mummy
case base

Mummy cover
(top and bottom)

Outer mummy case lid

Inner mummy
case lid

Gilded
top half

Wedjat
eyes

Painted
wood

**A MUMMY'S NEST**
This nest of mummy cases was made for
Henutmehit, a priestess in the Egyptian capital of Thebes
around 1250 BCE. The fine gold decoration suggests that she was
very important. Her mummy, which has not been found, would have
been protected by the mummy cover. This has an upper and lower
part, both made of cartonnage. The mummy was then laid into two
wooden cases, with the inner case fitting inside the outer one. Both
have eyes and eyebrows made of a black volcanic glass called obsidian.

Wood completely
covered in gold

22

# Mummy cases

AFTER AN ANCIENT EGYPTIAN HAD BEEN EMBALMED and bandaged, his or her body was placed in a coffin or mummy case. The case protected the mummy from wild animals and tomb thieves. More importantly, it was regarded as a substitute body and a house for the dead person's spirit. Mummy cases changed a lot through ancient Egypt's long history. The first ones were usually just plain rectangular wooden boxes. By the Middle Kingdom, about 2055 BCE, wealthy people were being placed inside two mummy cases for extra protection. Around the same time, the first mummiform (mummy-shaped) cases began to appear. By the New Kingdom, from 1550 to 1069 BCE, both inner and outer mummiform coffins were popular.

**EARLY MUMMY CASE**
About 5,000 years ago, an ancient Egyptian was placed in this reed basket and buried in the hot sand. Like a sand mummy (p. 8), he or she was laid in a hunched-up position with the knees tucked up by the face. But the basket stopped the sand from preserving the body, so only a skeleton remains.

**FINISHING TOUCHES**
This painting comes from the walls of the tomb of Ipuy, a sculptor during the reign of Ramses the Great (pp. 36, 50). It shows workers putting the finishing touches on Ipuy's wooden mummy cases.

**FACING THE RISING SUN**
A masked man called Ankhef lies in his rectangular coffin from around 2020 BCE. At some point he must have been turned around, because he should be lying on his left side, with his head on the headrest which is now by his feet. Mummies often faced east, so they could see the sun, a symbol of rebirth, rise over the desert each morning.

*Body wrapped in shroud*   *Headrest*   *False eyes*

**WRAPPED IN FEATHERS**
A vulture's feathers protect the owner of this mummy case lid. It is known as a *rishi* case, from the Arabic word for feathered.

**PAINTED EYES**
False eyes were painted on the east side of this wooden inner coffin (around 2000 BCE). Lying on its side, the mummy could "look out" through the eyes. Below them is a painted door, for the mummy's spirit to leave and reenter the coffin.

*False door*

*Continued on next page*

Outer coffin lid    Inner coffin    Masked mummy    Unwrapped mummy

## TINY NEST FOR A TINY MUMMY

This is one of two tiny nests of coffins found among all the treasures in Tutankhamun's tomb (pp. 38–39). It contained the mummified body of an unborn child, probably the king's daughter. The wrapped mummy was wearing a mask and lying inside a gilded inner coffin. All this fit inside a second, outer coffin less than 20 inches (50 cm) long.

## RED BRACES
The red braces on this inner case are a common feature of the period from 1000 to 800 BCE. They show that the owner was a priest or, as in this case, a priestess. The decorations in her hair are lotus blossoms (p. 30).

*Red braces*

*Sandaled feet*

Wooden case of priestess Katebet, from around 1300 BCE

## MUMMY CARGO

This tomb sculpture shows a mummy making the symbolic journey to Abydos, the city of the god Osiris (pp. 34–35).

# Why cartonnage?

Wood was the ideal material for making mummy cases. But there are very few large trees in Egypt, and the best pieces of wood had to be imported. An excellent alternative was cartonnage (p. 18), which was cheap, light, and easy to shape and paint.

## SEX CHANGE

This coffin's pink face shows that it was made for a woman. However, the inscription says the owner was a man, an official called Nesperennub, who lived around 800 BCE. Egyptians often took over other people's coffins in this way.

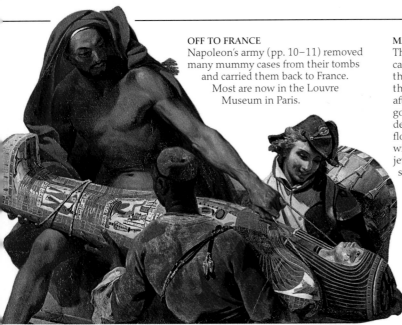

Detail from Léon Cogniet's paintings on the ceiling of the Campana room in the Louvre, showing one of Napoleon's soldiers transporting a mummy case

## MAGIC SYMBOLS
The symbols painted on cases were meant to protect the mummy or help it on the difficult voyage to the afterlife. In addition to gods and magic symbols, decoration included floral wreaths, elaborate wigs and collars, and jewelry. This is a selection of the most popular symbols.

*Wig*

*Collar ending in falcon heads*

*Scarab beetle on sacred boat*

*Sun*

*Red braces*

*Winged god with ram's head*

*Winged Uraeus, the royal cobra*

*Sokar bird*

*One of four Sons of Horus*

*Wedjat eye or Eye of Horus*

*Nut, the sky goddess*

*Winged falcon, sacred to the god Horus*

*Djed pillar*

*Shen, symbol of eternity*

*Anubis, god of embalming*

*Apis bull carrying mummy*

# Mummy case decoration

There is nothing sad or depressing about Egyptian mummy cases, which are painted in bright and joyful colors. This is because the Egyptians were confident that the dead person had left for a better world. Skilled artists painted the surfaces with beautiful hieroglyphs and religious images. Scenes from the Book of the Dead (pp. 12–13) were common. Other scenes show the Sun god Re, who the dead person was thought to join in heaven, or the scarab beetle, a symbol of rebirth (p. 44). The various gods associated with Osiris, in particular the four Sons of Horus (p. 20), were also painted on many coffins. Another popular figure was the sky goddess Nut, who is often seen on the lid or floor of the coffin, her feathery wings wrapped around the mummy in protection.

## SIDE VIEW
Pasenhor was one of the many Libyans who settled in ancient Egypt. This is his outer coffin, made of very thick wood, from about 730 BCE. The colorful decoration shows up beautifully against the white painted background.

## MUMMY BOARD
Mummiform boards were sometimes put on top of the mummy. This board of a priestess from 950–900 BCE is made of carved wood. This is covered by a layer of plaster painted in raised relief.

*Continued on next page*

# Later mummy cases

By the Late Period of ancient Egyptian history, mummy case production was a thriving industry. Ready-made coffins could be bought off the rack in a range of sizes and styles. Usually an inner, cartonnage case was fitted inside one or two outer cases made of wood. The surface decorations became more and more complicated, and large gods and goddesses were painted on the insides. Designs and hieroglyphs naming and praising the owner were often added to give each coffin a personal touch.

**WHAT'S YOUR SIZE?**
The largest outer cases are massive. Under three cases and layers of linen, the person seems tiny.

**BIG HEAD, BIG WIG**
The outer coffin lid of Nesmin from about 350 BCE has a huge head. This is sunk into rounded shoulders carrying a big wig and collar.

*Mummy with Ba bird*

**SURROUNDED BY GODS**
A woman named Seshepenmehit was buried in these two wooden coffins around 650 BCE. The floor of her outer coffin is decorated with a figure of the god Ptah-Sokar-Osiris, a symbol of birth, death, and the afterlife. Both coffin lids are covered in columns of hieroglyphs and scenes from the Book of the Dead (pp. 12–13).

*Hieroglyphs read "all life and power"*

**AND ON THE INSIDE…**
One of the earliest European pictures of an Egyptian mummy, this engraving was published by a French consul to Egypt in 1735. It shows how the pegs in a wooden mummy case join the lid and base.

**LACED FROM BEHIND**
Wooden mummy cases came in two parts, the lid and the base. But inner cases made of cartonnage were normally made in one piece. This cartonnage case from around 850 BCE would have held the wrapped mummy of a young girl. The mummy must have been placed inside while the linen was damp and flexible. Once the case had dried, its back was laced up like a corset, with thongs that sealed the mummy in. Only then was the case painted.

*Curved lid*

*Figures of Anubis*

*Corner posts*

**FOUR-POSTER**
Important officials who could not afford a sarcophagus might stretch to an extra outer coffin. The priest Hor (around 680 BCE) had two mummiform cases, which lay inside a large rectangular box. Also made of wood, this third coffin has a curved lid held up by four corner posts. Every inch of the cases is covered with gods, hieroglyphs, and magic spells.

**NOT MASKS**
These faces were carved from wood and pegged onto mummy cases.

*Cartonnage collar with falcon head at both ends*

*Apron, a painted body decoration*

*Face mask*

*Foot case*

**REST IN PIECES**
The Ptolemaic period began in 332 BCE, when Egypt was conquered by Alexander the Great (p. 29). The inner cases of Ptolemaic mummies consisted of four pieces of cartonnage—the face mask, collar, apron, and foot case. These were placed directly onto the shroud and then held in place with a last layer of bandages.

**THE LATEST FASHION, 200 CE**
In the Roman period, from 30 BCE to 323 CE, coffins were painted with their owners wearing daily clothes. This Roman woman left for the next world in a bright toga, worn with a stepped wig and a lot of jewelry, including gold rings.

*Ba bird*

*Hieroglyphs*

**SACRED BULL**
The ancient Egyptians worshiped many animals (pp. 44–47). The sacred Apis Bull was the largest and most important. There was only one Apis at any one time. He was kept in great luxury beside the temple, where he was attended by servants and a harem of cows. This painting on a foot board shows the bull carrying a mummy to its tomb.

**UNDER MY TOES**
Gilded sandals like these were sometimes painted under a mummy's feet. The figures painted under the mummy's sandals are tiny enemies, symbolizing the dead person's victory over evil.

*Colorful toga, a long piece of cloth wrapped around the body*

*Real rings stuck on fingers*

# Into the sarcophagus

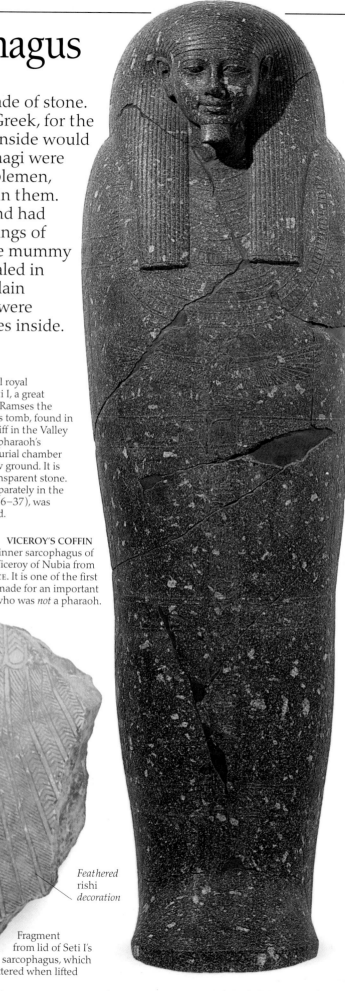

A SARCOPHAGUS IS A COFFIN made of stone. The word means "flesh eater" in Greek, for the Greeks believed that a body laid inside would be dissolved by the stone. Sarcophagi were expensive, and only pharaohs, noblemen, or important officials were buried in them. They were also incredibly heavy and had to be positioned in the tomb by gangs of workmen. During the funeral, the mummy was carried into the tomb and sealed in the sarcophagus. The first were plain rectangular boxes, but later ones were rounded to look like the mummies inside.

**HEAVY WEIGHT**
This huge sarcophagus of basalt is nearly 9 ft (3 m) tall and weighs 9,900 lbs (4,500 kg). It belonged to Wahibra, a scribe inspector.

**DIGNIFIED IN DEATH**
One of the most beautiful royal sarcophagi belongs to Seti I, a great warrior and the father of Ramses the Great (pp. 36, 50–51). His tomb, found in 1817, is cut deep into a cliff in the Valley of the Kings (p. 10). The pharaoh's sarcophagus was in the burial chamber over 330 ft (100 m) below ground. It is made of calcite, a semitransparent stone. Seti I's mummy, found separately in the royal cache of 1881 (pp. 36–37), was remarkably well preserved.

**VICEROY'S COFFIN**
This is the inner sarcophagus of Merymose, the Viceroy of Nubia from around 1380 BCE. It is one of the first stone coffins made for an important person who was *not* a pharaoh.

*Hieroglyphs, once inlaid with blue-green pigment*

*Feathered rishi decoration*

Fragment from lid of Seti I's sarcophagus, which shattered when lifted

Alexander
the Great

### ROYAL BATHTUB
The last real Egyptian pharaoh, Nectanebo II, was buried in this huge sarcophagus. It ended up in Alexandria, where the Greeks used it as a public bathtub. Before the hieroglyphics were translated, it was thought to have belonged to the Greek ruler Alexander the Great. Alexander's body has never been found, but ancient writings claim that he was preserved in a glass sarcophagus full of honey.

*Drain holes added for use as bathtub*

### BACK AT REST
Tutankhamun (pp. 38–39) is the only pharaoh still lying in his tomb. His mummy has been returned to its outer gilded coffin and laid back in the huge sarcophagus. This stone coffin was originally housed inside four gilded shrines large enough to house a car. Behind it are wall paintings showing sacred funeral rituals.

### PROFESSIONAL WEEPERS
Important Egyptians hired mourners for their funerals. These women would cry, wail, wave their arms, and throw dust in the air as the mummy was dragged into the tomb and laid in the sarcophagus.

Howard Carter (far left) watches as Tutankhamun's outer mummy case is lifted out of the sarcophagus

### WELL ARMED
This sarcophagus lid made of red granite covered the mummy of Setau, the Viceroy of Nubia. He was buried at Thebes around 1230 BCE. In his hands he holds two magical symbols, the girdle of Isis (p. 21) and the djed pillar (pp. 34–35).

### HOUSE OF SPIRITS
Like the oldest mummy cases, early sarcophagi were regarded as palaces for the dead. This rectangular sarcophagus made of red granite comes from the Old Kingdom, around 2500 BCE. At either end are false doors, for the mummy's spirit to pass through when it leaves and reenters the coffin.

*False door*

# Taking it with you

Slippers, makeup, a loaf of bread, a beautiful chair, some favorite earrings—the mummy had to be well prepared to enjoy life in the next world. Most of the artefacts that have survived from ancient Egypt were found in tombs, where they had been buried with the dead. Egypt's warm, dry climate has preserved many objects perfectly. Some mummies took the tools of their trade or symbols of their rank with them to the grave. Tutankhamun (pp. 38–39) was found with his childhood toys. Glamorous women were buried with their wigs, combs, fans, and mirrors. Musicians took along their instruments, and some people were even laid to rest with a board game, to while away the days of leisure in the afterlife.

*Corroded bronze surface, once polished for reflection*

**EARTHLY COMFORTS**
Sandals were a luxury, since most Egyptians went around barefoot. This padded leather pair is unusual. Most sandals were made from reeds found on the banks of the Nile.

*Makeup compartment*

*Sliding lid*

*Mirror with papyrus decoration on handle.*

*Sliding lid*

*Makeup box in form of stylized lotus flower*

*Cosmetic spoon in form of lotus flower*

*Cradle for head*

**FOREVER BEAUTIFUL**
Every mummy wanted to look good for the gods. Ancient Egyptian men, women, and children all wore makeup, particularly *kohl*, a type of eye paint. In addition to looking good, *kohl* protected against eye infections. Makeup was usually kept in containers decorated with lotus flowers and buds. The lotus, a type of water lily, was a sacred plant. The Egyptians saw its daily opening and closing as a symbol of life, death, and rebirth.

*Lotus stem*

*Ivory headrest, used instead of a pillow*

**STAY COOL**
In the hot climate, fans were a sign of wealth and sophistication. Pharaohs and other nobles even had special servants just to fan them.

### AT YOUR SERVICE
Model servants were placed in the tomb to look after the mummy's every need. This girl is carrying a tray of fresh bread. The walls of tombs were also decorated with paintings and sculptures of food, servants, and handy everyday objects. These were thought to come to life inside the sealed tomb.

*Brewer*

Coffin painting of dead person offering food to gods Re-Harakhty (middle) and Hapy (left), from around 1050 BCE

### DAILY BREAD
Coarse bread was an ancient Egyptian's staple food. Many mummies have badly worn teeth from eating it every day of their lives.

*Beer jars*

Figs placed in tomb 3,500 years ago

### BEER ON TAP
Ancient Egyptians were very fond of beer. By placing a model brewer in their tombs, they hoped to have a steady supply in the afterlife.

Harps were used to play hymns to gods in temple

*Pair of bronze cymbals*

*Drawer for holding the counters*

*Ivory board with 30 squares*

*Blue faience counters*

### THE GAME OF LIFE
Senet was ancient Egypt's most popular board game. Senet boards were placed in the tomb to symbolize the dead person's contest with evil to gain eternal life.

### ENDLESS JAM
This mummy may have been a professional musician who took his trusty cymbals with him to play in the next world.

*Ivory feather holder*

*Ostrich feathers, added according to paintings of fans found on tomb walls*

*Wood handle*

# Workers for the afterlife

**T**HE ANCIENT EGYPTIANS were an agricultural people, and every year they were all required to do some farming and irrigation work for the government. But rich Egyptians could avoid this work by paying someone to do it for them. When the mummy got to the Field of Reeds, as the Egyptians called heaven, he or she would have to do similar work, sowing and reaping for the god Osiris (pp. 34–35). So from early on, wealthy people were buried with model worker figures to do their work after death. In the early New Kingdom (about 1500 BCE), a single worker—or shabti—seemed to be enough to guarantee an easy afterlife. It was inscribed with Chapter Six of the Book of the Dead, which promised "O shabti, if the deceased is called upon to do any of the work required there... you shall say 'Here I am, I will do it.'" By 1000 BCE, rich Egyptians were being buried with 401 shabtis, one for every day of the year. The other 36 were bosses, armed with whips to keep the workers from slacking off as they sweated in the heavenly fields.

Overseer or boss shabti wearing skirt and carrying whip

**BOX OF WORKERS**
Shabti figures were often packed up in beautifully painted wooden boxes. This shabti box belonged to the priestess Henutmehit, whose golden coffins are on page 22.

**EARLY DIGGER**
Before the custom of shabtis, painted wooden servants and workers were placed in tombs. Unlike shabtis, this worker is not shaped like a mummy.

*Dead priestess gives offerings of food to gods*

*Gilded collar*

**WOMEN WORKERS**
These wooden shabti figures were both made for women from the 18th Dynasty, about 1550 to 1295 BCE.

Shabti of
Pharaoh Seti I

Nemes *headdress*

*Royal
cartouche*

*Cartouche,
oval-shaped
inscription with
king's name
written in
hieroglyphs*

Shabti of Pharaoh
Amenhotep III

Shabti of
Pharaoh Ahmose

**ROYAL SHABTIS**
The earliest surviving royal
shabti (above) belonged to
Ahmose, a pharaoh who died
around 1525 BCE. It is wearing a
*Nemes* headdress made from
cloth folded over the hair. Other
royal shabtis, like this one of
Amenhotep III (left), wear the
domed crown of Upper Egypt.

**ALL SORTS**
Stone, wood, clay, wax, bronze—
shabtis were made of all kinds
of materials. But the most
common was faience, a type of
earthenware heated up with
quartz to make
it look like tin.

**MODEL COFFINS**
Shabtis were sometimes put in elaborate cases
made to look like real mummy cases. This one
is made of blue faience.

**WELL EQUIPPED**
Many shabtis carry
hoes, picks, seed
baskets, and other
tools. These tell us a lot
about farming in
ancient Egypt.

*Pick*

*Hoe*

Lid of
inner
wooden
case on
right

Stone shabti in wooden mummy case and square outer coffin

# The mummy and the god Osiris

**T**HE GOD OSIRIS was said to have triumphed over death, and every ancient Egyptian wanted to follow his example. Legend told that far back in history, Osiris was a good pharaoh who was murdered by his evil brother, Seth. But his wife, Isis, and son, Horus, brought Osiris back to life. The story of the dead king's miraculous resurrection gave Egyptians hope in everlasting life. So to be reborn, a dead person tried to copy Osiris in every possible way. Mummies were prepared in exactly the same way as the body of Osiris had been long ago. If all went well, the mummy would "become an Osiris" and live forever.

Atef *crown*

Crook

Flail

Brightly colored coffin painting of Osiris wearing cobra crown and protected by falcons

Atef *crown made of two ostrich feathers*

Painted wooden statue of Osiris with green face and *atef* crown

Flail

Crook

**MUMMY AND SON**
The goddess Isis was the wife of Osiris. In this statue she is holding their son, Horus. The ancient Egyptians respected her as a devoted wife and loving mother.

**TOOLS OF THE TRADE**
These two statues of Osiris would have been placed in tombs or temples. They both show Osiris wearing an *atef*, a tall, feathered crown. In his hands the dead pharaoh is holding a crook and a flail. From the earliest times, the Egyptians associated these agricultural tools with kingship and justice. Osiris carried them when he sat and judged dead people's souls in the afterlife (p. 13).

**KEEP A STRAIGHT BACK**
The djed pillar is an amulet placed in the wrappings of a mummy (pp. 20–21). It was believed to represent the backbone of Osiris, and was thought to give the mummy strength after death.

Bronze statue of Osiris wearing *atef* crown

**FLAIL**
A wooden flail from a statue of Osiris. Like the sceptres carried by European kings and queens, the flail was a symbol of power and authority.

**GREEN FACE**
Among other things, the all-important Osiris was the god of vegetation and natural rebirth. In this role he was connected to the yearly flood of the Nile, which kept Egypt's lands green and fertile. Mummy cases often have green faces to link them with this aspect of Osiris.

*Lid with
falcon's head*

**CORN MUMMY**
It looks like a real mummy. But inside
the linen bandages of this mummy-
shaped model are grains of corn, not an
embalmed body. The corn "mummy" is
wearing a wax mask modeled to look
like Osiris. The Egyptians associated the
god with the success of the corn
harvest. Placed in a tomb, the corn
mummy would also help a real mummy
to join Osiris in the next world.

*Feathered* atef *crown*

*Wax mask
of Osiris*

*Royal beard*

*One of four
sons of
Horus*

*Hand holding
crook and flail*

*Djed
pillar*

**GROWING POWER**
The power of Osiris was
thought to be shown in the
sprouting of corn seeds.
Figures of the god were even
modeled in Nile mud and
sown with corn. This one was
found in Tutankhamun's tomb
(pp. 38–39).

# The royal mummies

THE FAMOUS PHARAOHS of the New Kingdom were buried west of Thebes (Luxor) in a desolate valley called the Valley of the Kings (p. 10). The tombs were cut deep into the rock. But despite all the precautions, they were robbed again and again in ancient times. Each time the priests had to rewrap the mummies and bury them again. Around 1000 BCE, they decided to group the royal mummies together and hide them in two caches (secret hiding places). The dead pharaohs lay hidden in these caches for nearly 3,000 years. The first cache was found in the early 1870s by three brothers who lived nearby. They kept it a secret and began to sell the treasures bit by bit. But the priceless antiquities were eventually traced to them, and in 1881 archeologists entered a deep tomb near Deir el-Bahari. They were amazed to find 40 mummies, among them famous pharaohs such as Seti I and Ramses II. The second cache, found in 1898, held another 16 mummies, ten of them royal. When this cache was shipped to Cairo, the customs officers at the city's gate had no idea how to classify it. In the end they decided to tax the dead pharaohs at the same rate as dried fish!

### INSIDE THE PYRAMIDS
The mummies of the kings who built the Giza pyramids have not survived. Despite their hidden entrances sealed with huge blocks of stone, these tombs were looted in ancient times. Once inside, robbers had to find the burial chamber in the darkness, along narrow passages full of false corridors and traps.

### LABELING THE KINGS
To avoid confusion, the priests wrote the pharaohs' names on the outer shrouds. This mummy is inscribed with the name Ramses III

### RAMSES THE GREAT
The famous Ramses II ruled for 67 years, from 1279 to 1212 BCE. He had a reputation as a great warrior, which he seems to have greatly exaggerated. He and his many wives had over 100 children, and he was probably in his nineties when he died. Ancient Egyptians were short by modern standards, around 5 ft 3 in (1.60 m) on average. But Ramses II's mummy, found in the 1881 cache, is 6 ft (1.83 m) tall (p. 50).

### REPAIR JOB
The mummy of King Saptah, who died in 1188 BCE, was badly damaged by tomb robbers searching for precious amulets in his bandages. The priests who moved him around 1000 BCE put his broken arm in a splint before rewrapping him.

Wrapped mummy of King Saptah as it was found in 1881

Unwrapped mummy of King Saptah

### GASTON MASPERO
This French archeologist (third from right) supervised the unwrapping of the royal mummies in Cairo. "And when I see, and touch, the bodies of so many illustrious persons we never imagined could be more than names to us," he wrote later, "I... find it hard to believe that I am not dreaming."

## MISTAKEN IDENTITY

This well-preserved mummy was found wrapped in a shroud inscribed with the name of Thutmose I (or Tuthmosis I). Examination of the mummy, however, suggests that it is someone else. Surviving historical records show that this pharaoh lived to about 50 years of age. The mummy belongs to a 30 year old man who seems to have died from an arrow wound to the chest so its true identity is still a mystery.

*Nemes headcloth, a sign of royalty*

*Wood covered in plaster*

*Remaining fragments of gold leaf*

## THUTMOSE I
A painting in a temple in Thebes shows the real King Thutmose I. This accurate copy was made by Howard Carter.

## GARLANDS OF FLOWERS
Flower wreaths were placed around a mummy's neck as it was laid in the coffin. When the lid of Amenhotep I's coffin was lifted, the sweet smell of flowers filled the room, 3,000 years after his burial. A wasp that had been attracted by the smell had been trapped in the coffin all those years ago. Its mummified body was found next to the king's.

*Ear of corn found in coffin*

*Fragments of wreaths placed on mummy*

## UNKNOWN QUEEN
Egyptologists are still not sure about the identity of this elderly woman with wonderful hair. Her mummy was found in the second royal cache of 1898. Some experts believe she is Queen Tiy, one of the wives of Amenhotep III, and probably Tutankhamun's grandmother. It was previously thought that she could be Queen Hatshepsut but in 2007 some Egyptologists claimed to have identified her mummy in the Valley of the Kings tomb, originally discovered by Howard Carter in 1903.

## ROYAL COFFIN
The mummy case of King Intef (from around 1650 BCE) is made from a hollowed-out tree trunk. This was plastered and covered with gold leaf engraved with a *rishi* feather design (p. 23). Robbers often stripped the gold leaf off royal coffins like this.

## A KING AT REST
The second cache of royal mummies was found in the tomb of Amenhotep II in 1898. Most of the mummies were shipped to Cairo, but Amenhotep was left lying in his sarcophagus where he had been found. Shortly after this photo was taken, a band of robbers overcame the armed guards and ripped open his bandages while looking for valuable amulets.

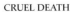

## CRUEL DEATH
The strangest body found among the royal mummies was this unknown man. His face is distorted with agony, and his mouth is open as if he were screaming. He must have died horribly, perhaps by being poisoned, suffocated, or even buried alive. His body was wrapped in a sheepskin, a material the Egyptians thought was unclean. No one knows what horrible crime he committed to deserve such a cruel death.

# The treasures of Tutankhamun

On NOVEMBER 26, 1922, Howard Carter peered through a small hole into a dark tomb in the Valley of the Kings (pp. 10, 36–37). "As my eyes grew accustomed to the light," he wrote later,"… I was struck dumb with amazement." The English archeologist and his wealthy supporter Lord Carnarvon had just discovered the tomb of the pharaoh Tutankhamun, sealed over 3,200 years before. Five years of methodical exploration had led them to the only fully intact royal tomb ever found—and probably the most exciting archeological discovery ever made. Inside was the king's mummy, wearing a superbly crafted mask of solid gold. The body lay in a nest of three gold mummy cases, each fitting inside the next. The cases rested in turn in a sarcophagus surrounded by four gilded wooden shrines and an amazing array of statues, furniture, and jewelry.

As Carter put it, it was a room full of "gold—everywhere the glint of gold."

Howard Carter (center) and his team stare in wonder at the sarcophagus through a door in the fourth shrine

**KING AND QUEEN**
The carving on this ebony and ivory box shows Tutankhamun in a garden receiving flowers from his queen. When his father, the powerful pharaoh Akhenaten, died, Tutankhamun was no more than nine years old. He probably never had much real power, and would barely be remembered if his tomb had not survived in such perfect condition.

**SCARAB PENDANT**
This pendant of a winged scarab beetle is made of gold and semiprecious stones. The design spells out the three hieroglyphs— Neb, Kheperu, and Re—of Tutankhamun's name.

*Gold sheets covering wooden frame*

Small shrine made to hold a sacred statue

*Decorated panels*

**THE KING'S DUMMY**
This painted wooden "dummy" shows the king as he must have looked when he died around 1327 BCE. It was probably dressed in the king's clothes and jewelry.

*Silver door bolts*

*Sled runners so shrine could be dragged into tomb*

*Shaved head*

*Bead vest*

**THE MUMMY**
The king's mummy was poorly preserved because of chemical reactions with embalming resins. He was slightly built and about 5 ft 5 in (1.65 m) tall. Studies of his teeth gave an age of 16 or 17. Despite claims that he may have been murdered, his actual cause of death is still uncertain. Latest research has dismissed the theory that he was struck on the head and suggested he may have died from complications following a leg injury.

Hunting scene

Nemes *headdress, a symbol of royalty*

Syrians

Tutankhamun in his chariot

Fan bearers

King's soldiers

Falcon-headed collar

### PAINTED BOX
This wooden box was stuffed with clothes, including the pharaoh's sandals. It is painted with scenes from Tutankhamun's life. On this side, he can be seen leading his army to victory over the Syrians, but it is unlikely that the king ever went to war. The painting is thought to be a symbolic representation of the pharaoh's supreme power. In two similar scenes on the lid, the young king hunts lions, ostriches, and antelopes in the desert.

### SLOW GOING
An Italian newspaper from 1924 tells the tale of the amazing discovery. Though he and Carnavon found the tomb in November 1922, Carter was so careful and painstaking in his work that he didn't begin to open the coffins until October 1925. It took him almost a decade to examine the entire contents of the tomb.

Inlaid lapis lazuli, a blue stone

### GOLD MASK
The king's mummy mask was made of solid gold inlaid with colorful glass and stones, including dark blue lapis lazuli. It weighed over 22 lb (10 kg). The pharaoh is wearing a *nemes* headdress (p. 33) and a vulture and a cobra sit on his brow.

### A NEST OF GOLD AND GEMSTONES
This is Tutankhamun's middle mummy case. Like the outer case, it was made of wood covered in gold and colored stones. It fit so snugly inside the outer case that Carter had a lot of difficulty lifting it out. Inside it was a third, inner case. This was solid gold and weighed an unbelievable 245 lb (110.4 kg).

Inlaid pieces of red, blue, and turquoise glass

Feathered *rishi design*

# Curse of the mummy

"**D**EATH SHALL COME ON SWIFT WINGS to him that toucheth the tomb of pharaoh." In the spring of 1923, newspapers around the world claimed that this dramatic inscription had been found inside Tutankhamun's tomb (pp. 38–39). The excitement was caused by the sudden death of Lord Carnarvon, one of the first to enter the tomb. Many people claimed that the dead pharaoh was angry and had "cursed" all those who had disturbed his rest. The curse has since been blamed for the deaths of many people connected with the discovery. Some now believe that the deaths may have been caused by bacteria or even atomic radiation sealed inside the tomb. But the deaths can all be explained, and the famous inscription never existed. Howard Carter and most of the others who entered the tomb lived on for many years. The most important wish of a pharaoh was that his name should live forever. Considering how famous Tutankhamun has become since his tomb was found, he should be pleased, not angry.

**MUMMY POWDERS**
Ground-up mummy was believed to have magical powers. It was used as an occult potion, and was a popular medicine in the 16th and 17th centuries. Powdered mummy was also used to make brown pigment for artists. The paint was called *Caput Mortuum,* Latin for "dead head."

**FIRST VICTIM**
Lord Carnarvon, Howard Carter's sponsor, had first come to Egypt because of his poor health. Early in 19.., he was bitten by a mosquito, and the bite became infected after he reopened it while shaving. A fever developed, and he died on April 5, 1923, just over four months after he and Carter had entered Tutankhamun's tomb. It was later said that the lights of Cairo went out at the moment of his death. Another story associated with the curse was that Carter's canary had been swallowed by a cobra on the day the tomb was opened. Tutankhamun's famous mummy mask has a cobra on the brow.

Lord Carnarvon's death certificate

Lord Carnarvon's cut-throat razor

Real mummy of Ramses III

Boris Karloff in *The Mummy*

**THE MUMMY BECOMES A MOVIE STAR**
The angry mummy disturbed from the sleep of centuries proved a great subject for horror films. The first was *The Mummy,* from 1932, which starred Boris Karloff as the mummified priest Imhotep (above). His appearance was based on the real mummy of the pharaoh Ramses III (left), found in the 1881 royal cache (pp. 36–37). In the film, Imhotep is brought back to life by a magic spell read aloud by an archeologist.

**DANGEROUS SPELLS**
This is one of four "magic bricks" that were found in the tomb of the priestess Henutmehit (pp. 22, 32). The bricks were placed at the four corners of the tomb and were believed to have supernatural powers. A spell from the Book of the Dead was inscribed on the mud surface of each brick. One of them reads "You who come to trap (steal), I will not let you trap… I am the protection for the Osiris Henutmehit." This was meant to keep away any intruders who might disturb the priestess's mummy in her tomb.

*Wooden figure attached to magic brick*

*Inscription in hieratic, a script that developed from hieroglyphics*

*Clay brick*

**THE MUMMY'S REVENGE**
Alongside *Dracula* and *Frankenstein*, the mummy bent on revenge became one of the most popular monsters in Hollywood horror films. This is a poster for a 1959 remake of *The Mummy*, made in color and starring Christopher Lee. The many other films included *The Mummy's Hand, The Mummy's Shroud, The Mummy's Curse, Blood from the Mummy's Tomb*—even a comedy spoof *Abbott and Costello Meet the Mummy*.

The archeologist's assistant in *Raiders of the Lost Ark* finds herself face to face with a tomb full of mummies

**LOST IN THE TOMB**
A newspaper story from 1934 tells of a Hungarian tourist who was lost in the tomb of Ramses II during a visit to the Valley of the Kings. She was found the next day, lying speechless at the foot of a statue of the pharaoh. Passing a night in the cold, pitch-black tomb had completely terrified her.

**SILENT SHRIEK**
Many mummy heads were collected in the 19th century and displayed as curiosities in European homes. Travelers to Egypt could buy them from dealers as part of a busy souvenir trade. This gruesome head was mounted under a glass dome. Nobody knows where it comes from, who it belonged to, or how old it is. Its grizzly features inspired some of the mummies used as props in the popular 1981 film *Raiders of the Lost Ark*. These were made of silicon rubber.

# Greek and Roman mummies

Many greeks had settled in egypt long before it was invaded by Alexander the Great (p. 29) in 332 BCE. Like the Romans who arrived in 30 BCE, the Greeks adopted the Egyptian custom of mummification. They took great care in wrapping their dead in elaborate geometric patterns. But beneath the linen, Greek and Roman mummies are usually badly embalmed. The mummies were laid to rest in open ground, not tombs, and several generations were often buried together in family graves. Some of the most interesting mummies from the Roman period were discovered in a cemetery in the Faiyum region of Egypt. Instead of having idealized faces like the ones found on Egyptian masks, they wear a realistic picture of the dead person. This sometimes takes the form of a plaster mask. But more often, portraits were painted on a wooden panel or straight onto the shroud.

**ROMAN CAT**
The ancient Greeks and Romans made mummies of all kinds of animals (pp. 44–47). This preserved cat is wearing a painted plaster mask. Two colors of linen bandages have been wrapped in an intricate "window" pattern.

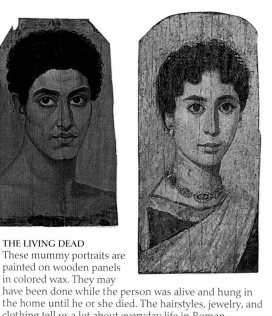

**THE LIVING DEAD**
These mummy portraits are painted on wooden panels in colored wax. They may have been done while the person was alive and hung in the home until he or she died. The hairstyles, jewelry, and clothing tell us a lot about everyday life in Roman-occupied Egypt around the time of Christ.

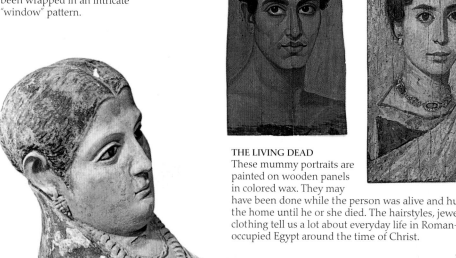

**PLASTER MASK**
Some Greek mummies wore plaster masks that made them look like they were sitting up in the coffin. Many of these masks are covered in gold and have inset eyes of stone or glass to make them look more realistic.

*Gilded studs*

**FOREVER YOUNG**
X-rays of this mummy of a Roman boy showed that he was in his early teens when he died. The elaborate bandages are decorated with gilded studs.

*Painted foot case*

**ROYAL BIRD**
The falcon soared to great heights in the skies of ancient Egypt. So it is not surprising that it became associated with the sky god Horus, who came to life as the pharaoh. In Greek and Roman times, falcons were mummified by the thousands and buried in special cemeteries with other sacred animals (pp. 44–47).

**DEATH OF CLEOPATRA**
Cleopatra, the last Greek ruler of Egypt, died in 30 BCE. Roman historians said that she committed suicide by holding a poisonous snake to her breast. Though there is no evidence to support the story, it has been painted and retold many times. Cleopatra's body was probably mummified and buried with all the ceremony due to an Egyptian queen. She was supposedly buried lying next to her lover, Mark Antony, but their tomb has never been found.

*Inscription in Greek*

*Figure of Osiris*

**MUMMY I.D.**
Mixing up the bodies in the embalming tent could have been disastrous. To avoid confusion, Roman embalmers tied a wooden label around each mummy's neck. In addition to the dead person's name, mummy labels are often inscribed with his or her age, profession, parents, even the date of death or where the mummy was to be buried. Some labels also carry a prayer for the dead person's soul, which relatives had bought instead of a tombstone.

**GOLDEN GIRL**
This Roman girl died in Egypt at the age of eight or nine. She was not properly embalmed, but her skin was coated in a dark, liquid resin to make it tough and waterproof. Her body was then covered in thin pieces of beaten gold. These were meant to connect her to the Sun god, who was thought to have flesh of gold.

Gold eye covers

Gold tongue cover

Gold nipple covers

**GOLD LEAVES**
The Romans placed pieces of gold over a mummy's sensitive parts. The tongue plate was probably meant to allow the mummy to speak.

Side view of Roman girl's head, showing eyelashes and gold leaf on face

*Pieces of gold leaf*

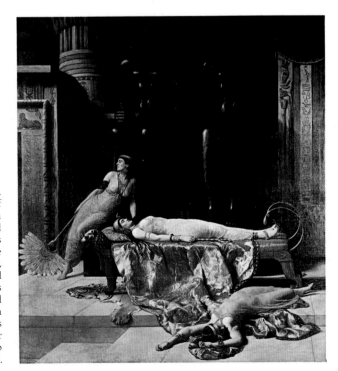

# Animal mummies

THE ANCIENT EGYPTIANS MUMMIFIED many animals with the same care they took for people. Favorite pets were occasionally mummified and put in the tomb with their owners to keep them company in the afterlife. But most beasts were embalmed for religious reasons. Animals were thought to be representatives or spiritual messengers of the gods. Many gods became naturally associated with one or more animals that shared the same qualities. The cow, for instance, which took such tender care of its young, was associated with Hathor, the goddess of love and motherhood. Special places became the centers of worship for major gods and goddesses. Here the animals sacred to these gods were mummified and buried in enormous cemeteries. By the later period of ancient Egyptian history, a huge religious industry flourished and millions of animals were bred just to be mummified.

**SACRED BULL**
When he died, the sacred Apis Bull (p. 27) was embalmed with the same care and ceremony shown to a pharaoh.

Bronze case for the mummy of a shrew mouse, sacred animal of the god Horus (p. 20)

Mummy of a wild dog or jackal, sacred to Anubis, the god of embalming (pp. 10, 13–15).

**PART EEL, PART SNAKE**
Bronze container for the mummy of an eel or cobra. The snake's beard and crown show its association with royalty.

**TWINS**
These two falcons were embalmed and mummified together, to strengthen their magical association with the god Horus (p. 20).

A limestone case for a mummified scarab beetle, the smallest creature to be embalmed

**ROLLING ACROSS THE SKY**
The scarab beetle rolls up balls of dung and pushes them around. The Egyptians believed the beetle god Khepri rolled the Sun across the sky in the same way.

Unwrapped mummy of a crocodile

*Linen bandages*

*Reeds used to pad out crocodile shape*

**ON THE MENU?**
An unwrapped mummified fish. Fish were sacred in some parts of Egypt, where they were never caught or eaten. In other areas, they were on the menu. This often led to violent conflicts between neighboring towns.

**IN THE NILE, CROCODILE**
In ancient times, the Nile River was full of crocodiles, which were feared for their ferocity. They were sacred to Sobek, a god of the water. Tame crocs were kept in luxury, fed on fine meats and wine and dressed in gold jewelry. The largest mummified crocodile ever found was 15 ft (4.6 m) long.

Painted plaster mask for a falcon mummy

Head of a mummified goose, sacred to the god Amun

**SACRED IBIS**
Three kinds of ibis were found in ancient Egypt. The migrant species with brown plumage still visits the country every year. But the bronze-colored crested ibis and the beautiful sacred ibis (right) are now extinct there.

*Head and neck made of bronze*

**SCRIBE GOD**
This gold container holds the mummified body of an ibis. Four million embalmed ibises were discovered at a single animal cemetery, each in its individual pot. They would have been dedicated to Thoth, the god of scribes and writing. Thoth was usually depicted with a human body and the head of an ibis.

*Wooden body covered in gold leaf*

**ROOST IN PEACE**
The mummy of a falcon lies in this coffin made of cartonnage (p. 18). The lid is richly painted with a floral collar and a winged scarab beetle. The designs are just like the ones on human mummy cases.

*Feet made of bronze*

*Prominent teeth*

*Geometric wrapping common in Roman period*

*Eyes, which bulge on top of crocodile's head*

*Continued on next page*

# The sacred cat

The graceful, green-eyed cats that leaped and purred around ancient Egyptian homes were a lot like the pets we keep today. Ancient Egyptian records show that cats were kept as pets as early as 2100 BCE. By the late period of ancient Egyptian history, the cat was a sacred animal. Writing about 450 BCE, the Greek historian Herodotus (p. 14) described how carefully cats were protected. Anyone who killed a cat could be punished by death. When a cat died, some families even took their beloved pet's body to the city of Bubastis, the center of worship for the cat goddess Bastet. Here the dead pet was embalmed, wrapped, and laid in a special cat-shaped coffin before being buried in a cat cemetery.

**CAT WRAP**
To mummify a cat, the embalmers began by removing its insides. Then they filled the pet's body cavity with dirt or sand and wrapped it in bandages that had been soaked in natron (pp. 14–15) or treated with resin. This fine mummy is wrapped in an elaborate diamond pattern.

*Green head symbolizes bronze mask worn by mummy*

*White body represents linen wrappings of mummy inside case*

Mummified cat

Cat mummy with comical face

**TIGHT FIT**
To produce a compact mummy, the embalmers laid the cat's front legs by its side and tucked its back legs up against its belly. The cat's tail was then curled up between its feet.

*Pierced ear, which probably once held a gold earring*

**BRONZE BASTET**
The yearly festival celebrating the cat goddess Bastet was one of the most important events on the ancient Egyptian calendar. This statue of Bastet made from bronze has inlaid eyes of colored glass. Many of these elegant figures wore gold rings in their ears and noses. Thousands of images of Bastet were set up in temples by priests, so worshipers could place offerings of food and milk before them. The priests also bred many cats specially for mummification.

Bronze container made to hold the mummified paw of a cat

*Wooden case with door at back*

**THE BALD TRUTH**
Shaving was seen as a way of cleansing the spirit, and ancient Egyptian priests and priestesses all shaved their heads. When a pet cat died, a whole household might go into mourning and shave their eyebrows as a mark of respect.

**PURR-SONALIZED COFFINS**
These wooden cat coffins were all found at Bubastis, the biggest center of cat worship. Each one contained the well-wrapped mummy of a cat. The largest one shows an idealized, graceful cat, but the other two are more natural and humorous. In the 19th century, some 300,000 Egyptian cat mummies were shipped to Liverpool in England, where they were turned into fertilizer and sold by the ton.

# Unwrapping the mummy's secrets

THE SCIENTIFIC STUDY OF MUMMIES does more than reveal how the ancient Egyptians embalmed their dead. Autopsies of ancient bodies can also show how people lived, what they ate, and what diseases they suffered from. In the 19th century, many mummies were unwrapped by surgeons. But their findings were limited by the technology of the age. Today, ruining the careful bandaging and dissecting the body is considered destructive and disrespectful. The invention of X-ray analysis in 1895 meant that mummies could be electronically "unwrapped" without being damaged. Early equipment was heavy and awkward. But by the 1960s, powerful, mobile X-ray units that could be brought into museums had been developed. The latest scanning equipment can "see" through the bandages and create complex, three-dimensional images of the body within. A small tissue sample from the mummy can be rehydrated (wet) and its cell structure studied. Even DNA, a person's basic genetic structure, can be identified. Some scientists believe that genetic analysis may one day help find a cure for modern viruses.

**CAIRO AUTOPSY**
Daniel Fouquet, a French doctor, unwraps the mummy of Tawedjatra, a priestess who died around 1000 BCE. This historic autopsy took place at the Cairo Museum in 1891. It was attended by the leading French Egyptologists of the day, along with several society women.

**ESTIMATING AGE**
This mummy of a man is lying in a coffin made around 1000 BCE for Tawuhenut, a female singer. Studies of his teeth and bones put his age at 20 to 35. More accurate estimates can be made for mummies who died before they were 25, when their teeth and bones were still growing.

**THE MANCHESTER TRADITION**
In 1908, Dr. Margaret Murray (second from right) and her colleagues unwrapped and dissected a mummy at Manchester University in England. They kept some tissue samples. These were examined in the 1970s as part of a major mummy survey led by Dr. Rosalie David. When rehydrated and viewed under a microscope, the tissues revealed evidence of a lung disease called silicosis. Desert sandstorms and the dusty climate may have caused breathing problems like silicosis for many ancient Egyptians.

_Artificial eyes_

_Scarab beetle amulet with wings wrapping around neck_

_Dense mass may be a pot_

## ALL IS REVEALED

This is a xeroradiograph of a mummy wrapped around 1000 BCE. Unlike normal X-ray images, xeroradiographs emphasize edges, so that outlines of shapes are easier to see. This is useful in identifying amulets (pp. 20–21) and wrapped organs, as well as bones and other body tissues. This image revealed a lot of packing material that was pushed under the skin to make the shrunken body more lifelike.

_Arms by sides (not crossed over) with hands covering genitals_

_Edge of linen bandages_

_Atef crown of two feathers, a symbol of the god Osiris_

_Facial features painted on wrappings_

_Ear wrapped separately_

## MALE DANCER

This unusual mummy from Egypt's Roman period (pp. 42–43) was found lying in the coffin of a woman dating from much earlier. From the packing, which emphasizes the shapes of the breasts and thighs, it was assumed that the mummy was female. But X-rays taken in the 1960s revealed a man's body beneath the wrappings. The paintings on the linen represent body tattoos. He may have been a dancer who performed at religious ceremonies and banquets, because such dancers are known to have had similar tattoos. The embalmers wrapped the mummy with great care, packing it to give it the shape of a living body. The facial features were painted on, in the style of Old Kingdom mummies. The fingers and toes are all wrapped separately, even in the outer layers. This is very rare.

_Elaborate geometric wrapping on forearms, typical of Roman period_

Side view of Roman mummy, showing careful wrapping of individual fingers

_Holes in skull_

_Badly bent bones_

_Tattoo painted onto wrappings_

_Piece of jewelry inset in sandal_

## BONE DISEASE

This cartonnage coffin from the 22nd Dynasty (945–715 BCE) once held the mummy of a child. All that remains of the body is a skeleton. Medical experts found that the strange deformities in the skull and other bones were caused by a rare bone disease called osteogenesis imperfecta. This would have afflicted the child while still in the mother's womb. He or she must have been born with brittle bones and probably died soon after.

_Linen sandals_

## MUMMY FINGERPRINT

Even after 3,000 years, it is still possible to take a mummy's fingerprints. Police forensic experts at Scotland Yard in London, England, have the prints of an Egyptian mummy in their records of modern criminals. They took the prints from a mummy's hand loaned to them by the British Museum.

_Continued on next page_

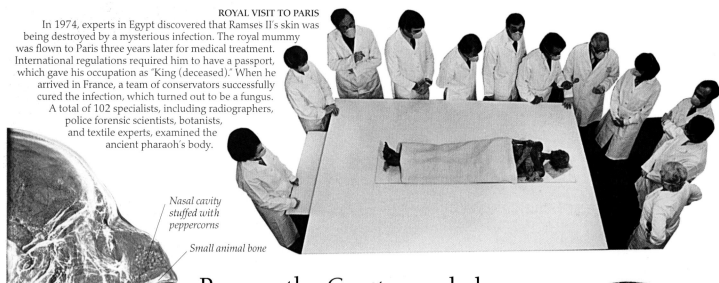

### ROYAL VISIT TO PARIS

In 1974, experts in Egypt discovered that Ramses II's skin was being destroyed by a mysterious infection. The royal mummy was flown to Paris three years later for medical treatment. International regulations required him to have a passport, which gave his occupation as "King (deceased)." When he arrived in France, a team of conservators successfully cured the infection, which turned out to be a fungus. A total of 102 specialists, including radiographers, police forensic scientists, botanists, and textile experts, examined the ancient pharaoh's body.

*Nasal cavity stuffed with peppercorns*

*Small animal bone*

*Missing teeth*

### STUCK UP

This xeroradiograph (a special high-definition X-ray) revealed the secret of the mummy's dignified profile. The embalmers had kept the king's nose in the air by packing it with peppercorns and propping it with a tiny animal bone.

# Ramses the Great revealed

The mummy of Ramses II was found in 1881 (p. 36) and has been resting in the Cairo Museum ever since. A special trip to Paris in 1977 gave medical experts from around the world a unique chance to examine the dead pharaoh's body. It is interesting to compare their findings with the historical records of his 67-year reign. X-rays showed a battle wound on one shoulder and signs of a healed fracture in one toe. The king may have suffered these injuries in recorded battles or from a hunting accident in the desert. Close examination revealed a tiny piece of blue and gold fabric stuck to the mummy's skin. This was probably part of the king's clothes. Traces of unusual sand suggest that he may have been embalmed near Per-Ramesse, the king's northern capital. Analysis of resins identified the herbs and flowers used to embalm him. Ramses' body was especially rich in camomile oil. It was also coated with an extract from a wild tobacco plant, possibly added to keep insects off the body.

### THE LIVING PHARAOH

This is Ramses II as he may have looked in life. Painted by Winifred Brunton in 1920, it was based on a comparison of his mummy and ancient sculptures. There is a striking physical resemblance between Ramses II, his father, Seti I (p. 28), and his son, Merneptah. The mummies of the three kings all have large, hooked noses.

### REDHEAD

Considering that he is more than 3,300 years old, Ramses II is in very good health. His hair was probably dyed with henna but seems to have been naturally red. His slightly open mouth reveals a good set of teeth. Abscesses in his jaw must have caused him great pain. The king also suffered from blood circulation problems and severe arthritis in the hips. This must have made it hard for him to get around in his last years. He was probably in his nineties when he died and had a bent back. To keep his head up, the embalmers had to break his spine.

# CT scanning

Since 1977, doctors have been examining mummies with the help of an advanced X-ray process called CT scanning. CT (also known as CAT) scanning is Computerized Axial Tomography (the last word means "cut" or "section"). A normal X-ray produces one flat view of an object, but a CT scan takes many thin views, each one like a slice of bread. These are then processed by a computer and put together to produce the whole loaf—a three-dimensional image of the object and all its surfaces, inside and out. It is possible to zoom in on one slice or isolate a particular part of the mummy to study it in more detail. The thickness of the slices can also be varied to give more information on one area like the skull or teeth. In 1991, doctors at St. Thomas' Hospital in London, England, began a mummy scanning program with the British Museum. The first mummy they studied was Tjentmutengebtiu, a priestess who died around 900 BCE. She is enclosed in a beautiful cartonnage case that would be damaged if it were opened.

Cartonnage mummy case of Tjentmutengebtiu

Artificial eyes

Winged amulet

Metal hawk-shaped amulet

Metal embalming plate

Metal amulet over genitals

Outline of mummy case

Winged metal amulet lying on feet

Mummy wrappings

Skeleton of mummy

## X-RAY VIEWING
The CT scanner can also simulate normal, flat X-ray images (above). Dense structures like bones are shown in white. Less dense materials like bandages come out dark blue or black. These X-rays show the skeleton inside the mummy and the mummy lying inside its case. The artificial eyes, various amulets, and an embalming plate can also be seen.

## TV CELEBRITY
Radiographers view the scanning process on high resolution television screens in a separate observation booth. They can control the thickness of the individual slices. The radiographers took slices 0.1 in (2 mm) thick of Tjentmutengebtiu's head and neck and 0.2 in (4 mm) thick for the rest of her body. It took a total of over 500 slices to scan the mummy from head to toe.

Dr. Stephen Hughes (left) and Dr. Ajit Sofat prepare the mummy of Tjentmutengebtiu to be CT scanned

## COMPUTER GRAPHICS
CT scans tell doctors a lot about the density of objects hidden beneath the surface. Different tissues like bone or skin have their own distinctive densities. Once these have been calculated, one tissue can be isolated from the others. This is the skin on Tjentmutengebtiu's skull. The doctors can even look inside her skull and see details like the sinus cavities. Information on density can also reveal if an object like an amulet is made of clay or metal.

# Mummies of the Andes

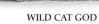

Dancing demon figure from Paracas, Peru, where many mummy bundles were found

THE EARLIEST MUMMIES FROM THE ANDES region of South America were made by fishing people who lived along the coasts of Chile and Peru. By 3000 BCE, they were preserving their dead by drying them in the sun and sometimes removing their internal organs, too. Mummies from various later cultures have been found all over modern Colombia, Ecuador, Peru, and Chile, from the high mountain peaks to the dry coastal lowlands. Many of these cultures treated the mummies of their ancestors as sacred objects. The Incas, who ruled most of the Andes region when the Europeans arrived in 1532 CE, believed their dead king was a god. By worshiping his mummy, they hoped to keep his soul alive. A dead king's mummy was seated on a throne and looked after by attendants who fed and clothed him. On important religious days, the royal mummies were carried through the streets of the Inca capital, Cuzco.

*Helmet*

*Mace*

*Shield*

**POTTERY WARRIOR**
The Moche were a farming and fishing people who lived on the northern coast of Peru from 200 BCE to about 600 CE. They made beautiful pottery to bury with their dead.

*Upper lip caught on tooth*

*Rope used to bundle body up*

*Well-preserved toenails*

**WILD CAT GOD**
Cloth was highly valued by the ancient Peruvians. They were great weavers and embroiderers who regarded cloth as a form of wealth. This tapestry of a cat god was woven by the Chancay people (1000–1470 CE). The Chancay did not have pet cats, so it must represent a wild cat like the puma or jaguar. Great quantities of colorful fabric were sealed inside tombs. Mummies were also wrapped in many layers of cloth specially made for the purpose. Fine quality garments were believed to show a person's importance. Weavers must have spent several years making the fabric for the most splendid mummies. Some burials even included cloth-making tools like looms, spindles, and thread.

**UNWRAPPED PERUVIAN MUMMY**
Some Peruvian mummies were carefully embalmed. This involved removing the internal organs, smoke-drying the body, and rubbing it with oils, resins, and herbs. But most mummies were preserved by natural conditions—either the hot dry climate of the coast or the freezing cold of the Andes Mountains. The drying process was probably aided by the layers of fabric, which helped draw off the body fluids. The dead person was usually placed in a sitting position with the knees drawn up against the chest. The hands were flattened over the face, and the arms and legs were bound tightly in place.

**DESERT CEMETERY**
The dry climate of the Peruvian coast was ideal for drying out mummies. In the 1880s, several hundred well-preserved mummies were found among the thousands of graves in the vast desert cemetery at Ancón. The high levels of natural salts in the soil seem to have helped preserve the bodies, including the mummies of pet dogs.

Male figure                Female figure

**FERTILITY OFFERINGS**
The Chancay people placed pottery with their dead. These hollow figures of a man and a woman stood on either side of a mummy. They were probably once wrapped in bright textiles.

**FALSE HEAD**
This is a false head worn by one of the mummies found at Ancón, Peru, in the 1880s. It is like a cushion made of painted cotton stuffed with leaves or seaweed. The nose and mouth are carved wood. The eyes are shells, with small drops of resin for pupils. The hair is made of plant fiber dyed black. This is wrapped in a headband and crowned with a headdress made of brilliant green parrot feathers. In ancient Peru, such headdresses were a sign of high status.

*Striped mantle (cloak)*

*Belt that pouches hang from*

**HIGH IN THE ANDES**
A side view shows the pouches that hang from a belt around the mummy's middle. They contain avocado pits, raw cotton, and coca leaves, which the Chimu chewed to relax. These leaves contain the drug cocaine.

*False head*

*Copper eyes*

*Copper nose and mouth*

*Feather eyelashes*

**MUMMY BUNDLE**
The Chimu were a highly developed farming people from northern Peru. Their kingdom flourished from 1000 CE until 1470, when they were conquered by the Incas. This is a Chimu mummy bundle with a false head. It contains a crouching body wrapped in many layers of fine cotton and wool cloth. X-rays revealed that the dead person's eyes were covered by plates of metal, probably gold. A bracelet was also seen on one wrist, and shells had been placed at the mummy's heels.

*Pouch*

*Continued on next page*

Continued from previous page

**False head**

**Wig of long strands of human hair**

**Leaf packing**

**Animal skin**

**Mantle**

### PARACAS NECKLACE

This cloth necklace was found in the desolate Paracas Peninsula, on Peru's south coast. Hundreds of mummies dating from 1000 to 200 BCE have been found in ancient cemeteries there.

*Tiny human figures*

### SACRED DOLL

found in the Pacasmayo Valley in Peru, this doll is made from woven tapestry, cloth, and reeds. She is clutching a bundle of raw cotton. Cotton was one of the first crops to be grown in the Andes, and evidence of it goes back to 3000 BCE. The doll may be a goddess buried with a dead person to bring him or her luck.

### INSIDE THE BUNDLE

This cross-section of a mummy bundle was drawn during the excavations of Ancón, Peru, in the 1880s. The mummy was found with a few vases in a grave 10 to 12 ft (3 to 4 m) deep. Its false head includes a wig of human hair. Beneath the layers of colorful cloth, the dried body had been wrapped in an animal skin and trussed up very tightly.

*Feathered headdress*

*Braided hair band*

### SNAKE EMBROIDERY

The Paracas Peninsula is famous for its ancient textiles, found either with or as part of mummy bundles. Some bundles contained over 100 cotton garments. Shirts, mantles (cloaks), ponchos, skirts, loincloths, and turbans have all been found. Many of them are embroidered in wool with birds, animals, fish, and imaginary beasts.

*Silver plate held between teeth*

*Cotton wrapping*

*Matting of raffia, a kind of palm*

*Stirrup spout*

*Turban*

*Ear spools*

*Feathered vest*

### BUNDLED UP

The Chancay culture flourished on the central coast of Peru from around 1000 CE to 1470. When ordinary Chancas died, they were wrapped in plain cloth and buried in simple pits with a few goods. But the rich were buried in great tombs, some with stairs leading down to them. These contained many rooms full of beautiful gifts. This Chanca woman was probably wrapped in palm matting. She is wearing clothes of cotton and feathers. Her mouth was packed with llama wool and sealed with a silver plate.

### MOCHE STIRRUP POT

The Moche made fine pottery vessels and figures specially to put in tombs. They even used clay molds to mass-produce favorite designs. The pots often have spouts shaped like stirrups. The head of a Moche lord forms the body of this pot. His ear lobes are stretched to take the large ear spools worn by important Moche men.

*Pair of gold ear spools*

*Sandals made of raffia fiber*

## SILENT SCREAM

Mexican museums contain many ancient mummies like this one. More recently preserved bodies have become tourist attractions. The gruesome mummies on display in Guanajuato, a vast cemetery in Mexico City, are all from the 20th century.

*Sewn-up eyes*

*Sewn-up mouth*

*Braided hair*

## SHRUNKEN HEAD

The Jivaro Indians of the Amazon were among the many groups of people who used to shrink their enemies' heads. They believed a person's soul lived in the head. By owning an enemy's head, a Jivaro warrior could possess some of the dead person's spiritual strength. They shrunk the heads to less than half their original size in an elaborate process that lasted six days. They then decorated the hair, which did not shrink, with beads and feathers. The result was a *tsantsa*, or trophy head. Warriors wore *tsantsas* around their necks at certain festivals.

# Other American mummies

Mummies have been found in many parts of the American continent, from Argentina in the south to as far north as Alaska. Some of the earliest bodies, from the first century BCE, come from the Kentucky region. Most of these mummies have been found in caves, like the bodies of Navahos in Arizona. The freezing cold has preserved the tattooed bodies of Inuit in Alaska. The inhabitants of the nearby Aleutian Islands buried their dead in warm volcanic caves that helped to dry them out. Some of the bodies found here were stuffed with dry grass after the insides had been removed. In South America, mummies have been found in many places beyond Peru. The Jivaro Indians of the Amazon even shrunk the severed heads of their enemies.

## CHILEAN GIRL

At its height, the empire of the Incas stretched from Ecuador in the north to Bolivia and Chile in the south. This is the freeze-dried mummy of an Incan girl found high in the Andes in Chile. The Incas practiced human sacrifice. During droughts or other times of crisis, children were sometimes selected, with their parents' approval, to be mummified and offered to the gods. When a king died, some of his favorite wives and servants were killed. They were then mummified so they could accompany the dead king on his journey to the next world.

## COLOMBIAN MUMMY

This mummy of a woman was found with 13 others in a cave near Bogotá, in the Colombian Andes. She is wearing a necklace of animal teeth and pieces of carved sea shell. Her internal organs were removed through an incision at the base of the spine. Her hands were then tied across her chest, after which her body may have been smoke-dried.

*Mark of tightly wrapped cloth on skin*

*Badly worn teeth*

*Dry, papery skin*

# The Iceman

ONE FALL DAY OVER 5,300 YEARS AGO, a traveler was surprised by a sudden snowstorm high in the Alps. He tried to shelter in a gully between two ridges of rock, but the storm was fierce, and he died where he lay from exposure and cold. Snow covered his body, and he was soon frozen into a glacier. Winters came and went, centuries passed, the empires of Egypt, Greece, and Rome rose and fell. Europe was ravaged by two world wars, but still the dead man lay frozen in time, until freak weather in the summer of 1991 exposed his body once again. A technique called radiocarbon dating was used to estimate the body's age. It showed that the Iceman, or Ötzi, as he is now known, died between 3350 and 3300 BCE. This makes him the oldest well-preserved mummy in the world. More than 70 objects were found with him, all personal possessions he was carrying when he died. Teams of specialists are now studying the Iceman's body, clothing, tools, and weapons. Botanists are examining the plant matter found on his body, which may show where he was traveling from. His blood, bones, vital organs, and DNA may reveal the diseases he suffered from. All of this research may give clues to who the Iceman was, and how he lived and died.

## THE DISCOVERY
On September 19, 1991, two German climbers found a body frozen in a glacier. It was about 10,000 ft (3,000 m) up in a remote part of the Alps near the Austrian-Italian border. The body had been partly uncovered because of a freak storm in the Sahara Desert in March. This had blown clouds of dust over the Alps and onto the glacier. The dark dust absorbed the sunlight and made the ice melt more than usual. Police and forensic experts who arrived on the scene didn't realize the body was so old. They hacked it out of the ice (above) and flew it by helicopter to Innsbruck, Austria, to be examined. At first it seemed that he was Austrian, and Austria has become the center of Iceman research. Surveyors later found that the body had been discovered just inside the modern Italian border.

## RADIOCARBON DATING
Robert Hedges works at the Radiocarbon Unit at Oxford University in England. He developed a new method of radiocarbon dating, which he used to prove that the Turin Shroud was a fake (far right). Radiocarbon dating works because all organic (living) things contain a molecule called carbon-14. This disappears at a constant rate after they die. So by measuring the level of carbon-14, scientists can calculate the age of any organic substance. Hedges dated the Iceman by testing a small bone sample. His results shocked experts, who had guessed that the Iceman had died around 2000 BCE.

## TURIN SHROUD
People once believed that the body of Christ was wrapped in this relic. But radiocarbon tests showed that it was made in the Middle Ages.

Leather quiver

Wooden ax with copper head

*Part of leather shoe lined with grass, still stuck on foot*

## ARMS AND THE ICEMAN
Some of the items the Iceman was carrying are extraordinary. There was a bow and a leather quiver holding 12 half-made arrows. His ax looks like a typical Bronze Age model from about 2000 BCE, but it turned out to be copper. It is an amazing tool, much older and more advanced in design than any known copper ax.

**BACK ON ICE**
Once removed from the glacier, the Iceman began to thaw and was in danger of decaying. A fungus had already started to spread across his body. Austrian medical experts removed this with great care. Then they refroze the ancient body in a giant fridge at 21°F (–6°C).

**TOOTH AGE**
Examination of the Iceman's teeth showed that he was probably in his late twenties when he died (p. 48). His teeth are badly worn, perhaps from a lifetime of eating coarse grain.

**FROZEN IN TIME**
So who was the Iceman? He was at least 5 ft 2 in (1.57 m) tall and had several strange tattoos. He was once well dressed for the mountains in patched leather clothes and shoes all stuffed with grass for extra warmth. He also had a grass bag and cape. In addition to an ax, bow, and arrows, he was carrying a flint scraper in a leather pouch. This may have been a kit for starting fires. What was he doing with all this gear so high in the mountains? He may have been a hunter or a traveler from a farming town on a trading mission. It is not clear in what direction he was crossing the Alps. He may have come from one of several known towns in Italy, Austria, or southern Germany.

# Bog mummies

**LINDOW WOMAN**
In 1983, two peat workers stumbled upon a partly decomposed female head, in the same bog in Cheshire, England where Lindow Man (p. 59) was later found. A local man soon confessed that he had murdered his wife and dumped her in the bog 23 years earlier. He was tried and found guilty of murder. But when the head was radiocarbon dated, it was found to be over 1,770 years old!

SOME ANCIENT BODIES have been found in wet, marshy places such as bogs. They are often found by people cutting peat, decomposed plant matter that has been burned as a fuel for centuries. The discovery of a body in a bog usually attracts the attention of the police, who assume that someone has had an accident or been murdered recently. Only after the body has been radiocarbon dated (p. 56) can scientists tell how long ago the person died. The best bog mummies have been found in northern Europe, especially Denmark. They date from the late Iron Age, as early as 500 BCE, to the Roman period, up to 400 CE. These well-preserved corpses have a number of things in common, and archeologists believe they are from a similar culture. The victims were all killed on dry land and then thrown into the bog. They may have been executed as punishment for some crime, or as a human sacrifice to the gods. Their many injuries even suggest that the victims were executed in some religious ritual. Forensic evidence suggests that they all died in midwinter, so this may have been a festival celebrated (like modern Christmas) at that time.

*Severed arm*

**HULDRE FEN WOMAN**
This bog woman was found over 100 years ago in Huldre Fen in Denmark. She died about 95 CE. Most bog bodies are naked, but she was wearing a lambskin cape and a checked skirt and head scarf. A finely crafted horn comb and a string with two amber beads were also found with her. This suggests that she was not poor and may have held an important position in society. No one knows if her arm was cut off before or after she died.

*The hair of many mummies seems to have turned red over the years*

*Scar from cut throat*

**GRAUBALLE MAN**
This body of a man was found near Grauballe, Denmark, in 1952. At first he was thought to be a drunken peat worker known as Red Christian, who had fallen into the bog way back in 1887. Analysis of the hair and radiocarbon dating of the body suggest that he died between 400 and 200 BCE. The body had to be treated to stop it from deteriorating after it was taken from the bog. It was placed in a strong solution of oak bark and slowly tanned over 18 months. Grauballe Man is incredibly well preserved, with most of his internal organs intact. Even his fingerprints could be studied (p. 49). The contents of his stomach told scientists what he had eaten for his last meal. He seems to have had a vegetable soup with barley and a sort of muesli made from the seeds of over 60 different plants. He died violently from many injuries, including a slit throat.

*Long, narrow hand*

*Leathery skin, naturally tanned in peat bog*

## OVERKILL
Lindow Man seems to have been killed by several methods. A knotted cord was found embedded in his neck. It seems to have been used to choke or strangle him. His throat was also slit, and his skull was caved in by heavy blows. All this "overkill" suggests that his death was a sacrifice or some kind of religious ceremony.

*Fragile hair, including a beard, rarely found on bog bodies*

*Cord used to choke or strangle him*

## AGREEING ON A DATE
Bogs contain little oxygen. This stops bacteria, which cause decay, from growing (p. 8). How well a body is preserved also depends on how cold the water is and how deeply the body is submerged. A team of archeologists and other specialists removed Lindow Man from the peat. They then took samples from the body and the peat and sent them to three research laboratories to be dated by the radiocarbon method. Though their results were not identical, the experts eventually agreed that the Lindow Man had died around 300 BCE.

*Ulna, one of the bones in the forearm*

*Fingernail resting on skin*

*Fragments of bones from right hand*

*Navel*

*Tough, leathery skin*

## WHAT DID HE LOOK LIKE?
Lindow Man must have looked a lot better 2,300 years ago. But lying crumpled in his wet grave, his face was distorted over the centuries. This was a challenge for scientists who try and reconstruct faces to help the police to identify human remains. They base their calculations on careful measurements of the skull, allowing for the thickness of skin and muscle. The fine condition of his fingernails shows that Lindow Man didn't work with his hands, and may even have been a chieftain.

# Lindow Man

In 1984, peat cutters found a man's body in a bog at Lindow Moss in Cheshire, England. The discovery that he was about 2,300 years old made the dead man famous overnight. Newspapers gave him the nickname Pete Marsh, a pun on the type of bog he was found in. Scientific research revealed many interesting details about his body. Examination of his teeth suggests he was between 25 and 30 years old when he died. He was in good health, but suffered from intestinal worms. The contents of his stomach showed that his last meal was a high-fiber mixture of cereal, bran, and slightly burned bread.

# The mummies of Sicily

ABOUT 6,000 MUMMIES are still resting in a catacomb (underground cemetery) beneath a Catholic church in Palermo, the capital of the Italian island of Sicily. The first mummies, nearly 400 years old, are of monks who lived and worshiped in the church. The custom soon became fashionable with doctors, lawyers, and other rich professionals in Palermo. The monks embalmed the bodies themselves, in a secret process that took more than a year. Like the ancient Egyptians, the Sicilians didn't find their mummies disturbing. They saw the preserved bodies as a direct link with their dead relatives, whose spirits were enjoying the afterlife. Families took their children to visit their great grandparents, long after they had passed away. Visitors brought picnics on their outings to the catacombs. The families would pray and talk to the mummies, keep them up-to-date on local affairs and ask their advice on difficult matters. No one has been mummified for over 80 years, but the monks are still kept busy giving tours to visitors from far beyond Sicily.

**FOUNDING FATHER**
The oldest mummy in the catacombs is Father Silvestro da Gubbio, embalmed in 1599. First, his body was carried down to a special cellar, the *collatio*. Here it was laid on earthenware pipes and left for 12 months, until all the body fluids had drained away. It was then taken upstairs and left to dry in the sunshine. Before it was dressed, the body was washed in vinegar and wrapped in straw and sweet-smelling herbs.

**BEARDED GUARDIANS**
The monks live over the catacombs and are in charge of the mummies and all the cemetery records. They belong to the Capuchin order. All Capuchin monks have beards and wear robes with hoods.

**DRESSED IN SUNDAY'S BEST**
These mummies of women are all from a part of the catacombs known as the Corridor of the Virgins. Their costumes are a remarkable historical record of dress-making skills and textile design. The lacework is particularly impressive. The coffins the bodies lie in are hinged, so relatives could hold hands with the mummies while they prayed.

*Well-preserved, colorful clothes*

*Labels with details like the dead person's name, age, and profession*

**MILKY SOFT**
In the 19th century, a new, better method of embalming was developed. The monks began to soak the bodies in arsenic or milk of magnesia, which left the skin softer and more lifelike.

**DUSTY DEATH**
There are now fewer than 40 monks looking after the 6,000 mummies. Every year, they give the dead bodies a gentle clean with a vacuum cleaner.

*Clothes of cotton, which has worn away less than silk*

Sicilian mummy with head propped up on pillow

**SLEEPING BEAUTY**
Rosali Lombardo, the last Sicilian to be mummified, died at the age of two in 1920. Her body was preserved by a unique process developed by her father, who was a doctor.

# Other mummies

### GUANCHE MUMMIES
In 1770, a volcanic cave containing about 1,000 mummies was found on Tenerife, one of the Canary Islands. They belonged to the Guanche people, who had been preserving their dead for centuries. Their method of embalming was remarkably like the Egyptian way. In some cases the Guanches removed the internal organs. Then they dried the body and stuffed it with plants. Few Guanche mummies have survived, because so many were ground up to make medicines.

N ATURAL MUMMIES ARE PRESERVED by accident (pp. 8–9) and are found anywhere in the world where it is cold, dry, or marshy enough. Australian Aborigines, Torres Strait Islanders, and Native Americans all used natural conditions to preserve bodies deliberately. In Christian churches and Buddhist temples, holy people are sometimes mummified and put on display (pp. 7, 60–61). Every year, the mummy of a Christian saint is carried through the streets in a great procession in a town in Crete. In the 20th century, people began to mummify famous politicians and celebrities rather than kings and saints. Improved methods of embalming involving paraffin wax were developed in Argentina. In 1952, these were used to preserve beautifully the body of the president's wife, Eva Perón. In Salt Lake City, you can now pay to have a dead relative or pet embalmed and wrapped in the ancient Egyptian way.

*Wax head*

*Real head*

### AUTO ICON
When the English philosopher Jeremy Bentham died in 1832, he left his body to a surgeon friend. According to his instructions, his head was mummified. His skeleton was then dressed in his everyday clothes and crowned with a wax head. The whole ensemble is still displayed in a glass case in University College, London. Bentham called it his "Auto Icon" (self-image).

### FISHY MUMMY
Mermaids (and, more rarely, mermen) were popular curiosities in Europe as early as the 17th century. These imaginary creatures mostly came from East Asia, especially Japan. This mummified merman was made from a monkey's body and a fish's tail. Seijiro Arisuye, who gave it to an English prince, claimed that it had been caught by a Japanese fisherman.

*Sealskin trousers*

*Outer parka made of sealskin trimmed with fur*

*Kamik, sealskin boots*

## LADY DAI, HER TRUE STORY

Lady Dai was a Chinese noblewoman from the Han dynasty who died around 168 BCE. Her well-preserved body was found in a deep tomb in Hunan province in 1972. She was wrapped in 20 layers of silk and lay in a nest of six wooden coffins, all beautifully painted. These were covered in many layers of bamboo matting and five tons of charcoal. This was probably designed to soak up any water and keep the body perfectly dry. The tomb was then sealed with dirt and clay to keep it airtight. Examination of her body showed that Lady Dai had been embalmed by soaking in a bathtub of mercury salts.

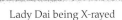

Lady Dai being X-rayed

*2,160 pieces of nephrite, a kind of jade, linked with gold wires*

## SUN DRIED

This New Guinean is posing proudly with a mummified ancestor. In hot parts of the world, many people used to place bodies in the branches of trees to be dried by the sun. The islanders of the Torres Strait, between Australia and New Guinea, would tie a dead body to a bamboo stretcher. Then they would light a fire under it and smoke it dry. Finally they painted the body with red ocher.

## JADED SUIT

A Chinese princess from the second century BCE was buried in this beautiful jade suit. She had hoped that the gemstone would mummify her. But under the jade, her body decayed anyway.

## FROZEN SCYTHIANS

The Scythians were nomads who ruled central Asia from the seventh to the third century BCE. They mummified their dead chiefs and nobles with as much care as the ancient Egyptians. They removed the internal organs and stuffed the body with frankincense, parsley, and hair. This picture of a Scythian horseman is part of a textile buried with a chief. The Scythians spent most of their lives on horseback, and chiefs were even buried with their mummified horses. Warriors were tattooed for their bravery. Their burial mounds in Siberia were freezing cold, which helped to preserve the bodies.

## DRESSED IN FURS

This mummy of an Inuit woman is one of eight well-preserved bodies found in Greenland in 1972 (p. 7). She died around 1475 at the age of 30. The combination of dry air and freezing temperatures naturally freeze-dried her body. Her warm clothing, all handmade from animal skins, was also well preserved. The Inuit believed that a dead person's soul would need warm clothes for the long voyage to "The Land of the Dead." Infrared photographs revealed faded tattoos on her face. Four of the other five women buried with her had similar tattoos.

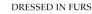

*Inner parka made of bird skin*

# Did you know?

## AMAZING FACTS

Chancay doll

The Chancay people from South America often placed doll-like figures in their tombs to serve the dead person in the afterlife, much like Egyptian shabti figures.

Canopic jars, used to store a mummy's internal organs, are named after the local god of Canopus, a town in the Nile delta region. He was represented as a human-headed pot.

The ancient Egyptians believed that the land of the dead lay in the west, where the Sun set, so most of their cemeteries, including the Valley of the Kings, were situated on the west bank of the Nile River. One of the names for Osiris, the god of the dead, was "Foremost of the Westerners."

The Egyptian god Osiris

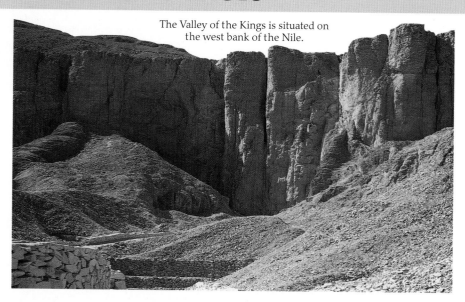

The Valley of the Kings is situated on the west bank of the Nile.

In ancient Egypt, a body being mummified was placed on a slanted bed and covered with a form of salt called natron for 40 days. At the end of this period, the body would have shrunk in size and lost about 75 percent of its original weight, thanks to the dehydrating effect of the natron.

The frozen bodies of sailors from Sir John Franklin's Arctic expedition of 1845 were so well preserved that scientists were able to perform post-mortems. The results suggested that lead poisoning, caused by eating badly canned food, may have caused the mental and physical decline of the crew.

Egyptologists gained useful information about the process of mummification from an account in the Bible. In the book of Genesis, Jacob dies in Egypt and his son Joseph has his body embalmed. "So the physicians embalmed him, taking a full 40 days, for that was the time required for embalming. And the Egyptians mourned him for 70 days." (Genesis 50:2–3). These 40- and 70-day periods confirmed another account given by the Greek historian Herodotus.

Vast amounts of linen were used to wrap an ancient Egyptian mummy. When experts at the Metropolitan Museum of Art in New York measured how much linen had been used on one mummy from the 11th dynasty, they found that it totaled an amazing 9,095 square feet (845 square meters). That's enough linen to cover three tennis courts!

During mummification, the internal organs were removed through a long incision on the left side of the body. The line of the cut was marked by one priest, called a "scribe," then a second priest, appropriately known as the "slicer" or "ripper up," made the cut with a flint knife.

During the Middle Ages, mummies were in great demand in Europe for use as medicine. Large numbers of them were imported from Egypt for this purpose. One common use was to boil a mummy and then skim off the melted oils to make an ointment to stop bruising. Mummy was also used as an ingredient in potions to treat stomach upsets and many other illnesses.

The Valley of the Kings was said to be protected by a goddess called Meretseger, who took the form of a cobra. The tomb workers believed that she would blind or poison any robbers who tampered with the tombs.

The goddess Meretseger, in the form of a cobra

Step Pyramid

**Q** Why were early Egyptian pharaohs buried in pyramid-shaped tombs?

**A** The earliest pyramid was the Step Pyramid, built as the burial place of King Djoser in around 2650 BCE. Its shape was supposed to represent a giant stairway for the dead king to climb to join the Sun-god in the sky. Later pyramids had sloping sides. This shape represented the mound which, according to Egyptian legend, had emerged from the watery ground at the beginning of time. The Sun-god stood on the mound and brought the other gods and goddesses into being.

**Q** Why didn't the Egyptians remove a mummy's heart?

**A** Egyptian embalmers removed most of a mummy's internal organs, but the heart was always left in place. The Egyptians believed that the dead person would need his or her heart when they were judged in the afterlife (see p. 13). It was therefore essential that the heart was kept with the body, and it was often protected by a powerful amulet, called the heart scarab.

*Anubis, jackal-headed god of embalming*

Egyptian god Anubis

**Q** Why was the Egyptian god Anubis associated with mummification?

**A** Real jackals often roamed the graveyards of ancient Egypt, so this is probably why Anubis, the jackal-headed god, came to be the god of embalming and the guardian of the dead. He was often depicted with black skin, because for the Egyptians the color black represented the fertile Nile mud and, therefore, life itself.

**Q** Are bodies still being mummified today?

**A** Yes, but in different ways. You can have your dead pet mummified, and some wealthy people have their bodies preserved using a form of deep-freezing, called cryonics.

**Q**  Were the dead always treated with respect?

**A** Egyptian embalmers were not always as careful as they should have been when preparing mummies. We know of one mummy whose head snapped off and was reattached to the body with a stick, and a queen whose face was so stuffed with pads of linen that it split away from her head. Once the body was wrapped in bandages, the grieving family could not see these mistakes.

**Q**  What happened to Egyptian tomb robbers if they were caught?

**A** Egyptian pharaohs were buried with such vast amounts of treasure that their tombs inevitably attracted robbers. If they were lucky and escaped undetected, tomb robbers could make quick profits from selling their loot, but if they were caught, they faced a terrible fate. First, they would be tortured by having the soles of their feet beaten with rods. Then they would suffer an agonizing public death, impaled on a sharp wooden stake.

**Q**  Which animals were mummified?

**A** The ancient Egyptians mummifed all kinds of animals. Cats, rams, ibises, hawks, and crocodiles were among the most common, but mice, rats, lizards, and even a mummified egg have also been found.

## Record Breakers

**OLDEST WELL-PRESERVED MUMMY**
The body of the Iceman was preserved in a glacier in the Alps for more than 5,300 years (see pp. 56–57).

**MISSING MUMMY**
In 1818, the Italian archeologist Giovanni Belzoni entered the burial chamber of the Great Pyramid. He discovered that it had been robbed, and there was no sign of the mummy of Pharaoh Khufu. The mummy has never been found.

**RICHEST MUMMY**
Not only was Tutankhamun the only royal mummy discovered with its priceless treasures intact, but his treasures continued to earn vast amounts of money when they went on tour around the world during the 1960s, 1970s, and 2007–2009. The exhibition has proved so popular that visitors often stood in line for hours to see it.

**MOST POPULAR MUMMY?**
Millions of visitors to Moscow have been to see the mummified body of the Russian leader Vladimir Lenin making him one of the city's most popular tourist attractions.

The frozen, naturally mummified body of the Iceman was found in the Alps.

# Timeline

THE PRESERVATION of dead bodies by mummification has been happening for centuries. Sometimes it is accidental—by favorable weather conditions, while others have been deliberately preserved by people. The mummies in this book span more than 5,000 years, from the Iceman, who died around 3350 BCE, to Lenin, whose body was mummified in the 1920s.

*These figures were probably a mother and her child*

Casts of two bodies, whose shapes were preserved in the ash at Pompeii

**c. 3350–3300 BCE EUROPE**
A traveler later known as the "Iceman" dies of exposure and cold in the Alps. His body is frozen into a glacier.

**c. 3200 BCE EGYPT**
The oldest surviving Egyptian mummies date from this period. They are bodies buried in the desert sand, which dries and mummifies them naturally.

**c. 3000 BCE SOUTH AMERICA**
People along the coasts of Chile and Peru preserve the bodies of their dead by drying them in the sun. Some claim that small fishing communities there known as the Chinchorro started this practice as early as around 6000 BCE.

**2686–2160 BCE EGYPT**
During the Old Kingdom, mummies of kings and queens are buried in pyramids.

A 2000-year-old mummy from Peru, preserved by dry conditions

**c. 2000 BCE EGYPT**
The Egyptians start embalming some of the body's internal organs separately and storing them in canopic jars. The first mummiform (mummy-shaped) coffins are used.

**1492 BCE EGYPT**
Death of Pharaoh Thutmose I (aka Tuthmosis I), the first pharaoh to build his tomb in the Valley of the Kings.

**1327 BCE EGYPT**
Death of the boy pharaoh, Tutankhamun. He is buried in a small tomb in the Valley of the Kings.

**c. 1000 BCE EGYPT**
Egyptian priests collect a number of royal mummies from tombs in the Valley of the Kings that have been disturbed by robbers. They rebury them in two secret hiding places, called caches.

**450 BCE EGYPT**
The Greek historian Herodotus visits Egypt and writes an eyewitness account of the mummification process.

**c. 300 BCE ENGLAND**
A man is sacrificed during a religious ceremony and his corpse is thrown into a bog at Lindow Moss in Cheshire.

**79 CE ITALY**
Mount Vesuvius erupts, burying the nearby towns of Pompeii and Herculaneum under volcanic rock and ash. The ash forms a hard crust around each body. Once the bodies decomposed, empty body-shaped spaces were left in their place.

**c. 1000–1476 SOUTH AMERICA**
The Chimu people rule northern Peru. They mummify their dead and bury them in mummy bundles.

**c. 1100–1532 SOUTH AMERICA**
The Inca people rule an empire stretching from modern-day Ecuador to Chile and Bolivia. They bury their dead in the Andes Mountains. The bodies are mummified by the cold, which freeze-dries them.

Mummy of an Inuit child, preserved by dry air and icy temperatures

**c. 1475 GREENLAND**
The bodies of eight Inuit people are freeze-dried by dry air and freezing temperatures. They are not discovered until 1972.

**1599 ITALY**
Monks at a church in Palermo, Sicily, start mummifying the bodies of monks who die. The practice continues until the 1920s.

Mummified bodies in a church
in Palermo, Italy

## 1984 THE ARCTIC
The bodies of three sailors from Sir John Franklin's 1845 expedition are discovered in the Canadian Arctic. The icy conditions have preserved their bodies intact.

## 1984 UK
The body of "Lindow Man" is discovered preserved in the Lindow Moss bog. The body has been lying there for 2,300 years, but scientists are able to establish how he died, how old he was, and what he ate for his last meal.

## 1991 EUROPE
Freak weather conditions in the Alps expose the body of the Iceman. Scientists use radiocarbon dating to eastablish that the body has been frozen in the ice for over 5,300 years.

## 1798 EGYPT
Napoleon Bonaparte invades Egypt. French scholars remove many mummy cases from their tombs and send them to Paris.

## 19TH CENTURY JAPAN
The bodies of some Buddhist priests are mummified by smoke-drying.

Engraving of Sir John Franklin's
expedition to the Arctic

## 1845 THE ARCTIC
Sir John Franklin leads an expedition along the northern coast of Canada, looking for a route to the Pacific. Franklin and his men are never seen alive again.

## 1880s SOUTH AMERICA
Several hundred ancient Peruvian mummies are found in a vast desert cemetery at Ancón.

## 1881 EGYPT
A cache of royal mummies is discovered at Deir el-Bahari, near the Valley of the Kings. It contains 40 royal mummies, including the famous pharaohs Seti I and Ramses II.

## 1898 EGYPT
A second cache of mummies is discovered in the Valley of the Kings in the tomb of Amenhotep II. It contains 16 mummies, 10 of them royal.

## 20TH CENTURY MEXICO
Large numbers of mummified bodies are buried in the Guanajuato cemetery in Mexico City.

## 1922 EGYPT
Archeologist Howard Carter discovers the tomb of Tutankhamun in the Valley of the Kings. It contains many treasures and his mummy— the only pharaoh's mummy ever found undisturbed in its tomb.

## 1924 RUSSIA
Death of the Russian revolutionary leader Vladimir Lenin. His body is preserved using paraffin wax and displayed in Red Square, Moscow.

## 1950 DENMARK
The 2,000-year-old body of a man is discovered preserved in the Tollund bog.

## 1977 FRANCE
The mummy of Pharaoh Ramses II is taken to Paris for X-rays and other tests.

Mummified body of Lenin

## MAIN PERIODS IN EGYPTIAN HISTORY

The civilization of ancient Egypt lasted for more than 3,000 years. Historians divide this huge length of time into various periods, which are listed below. They also group the pharaohs into "families" of related kings, called dynasties.

c. 3100–2686 BCE Early Dynastic Period
1st–2nd dynasties

c. 2686–2181 BCE Old Kingdom
3rd–6th dynasties

c. 2181–2055 BCE 1st Intermediate Period
7th–10th dynasties

c. 2055–1650 BCE Middle Kingdom
11th–14th dynasties

c. 1650–1550 BCE 2nd Intermediate Period; 15th–17th dynasties

c. 1550–1069 BCE New Kingdom
18th–20th dynasties

c. 1069–747 BCE 3rd Intermediate Period
21st–24th dynasties

c. 747–332 BCE Late Period
25th–30th dynasties

c. 332–30 BCE Ptolemaic Period
Macedonian and Ptolemaic dynasties

# Find out more

IF YOU ARE LUCKY ENOUGH to be going on a trip to Egypt, you will have no trouble seeing lots of mummies, and you will also be able to visit the pyramids and tombs where they were buried. But you don't have to travel that far to find out more about mummies. Many museums have mummies from Egypt and South America on display, so check out your local museum to see if it has a collection worth visiting. Alternatively, you could unwrap the secrets of mummies from your own home. Visit some of the exciting websites devoted to mummies, and keep an eye open for documentaries about mummies on television.

*Headdress of the ram-headed god, Khnum*

Visitors inspecting a mummy in the Egyptian Museum, Cairo

**VISITING EGYPT**
Many famous royal mummies now lie in the Egyptian Museum in Cairo (see below), while the Mummification Museum at Luxor (Thebes) is home to many human and animal mummies. Another site worth visiting is the Serapeum, near the Pyramids at Giza, where the mummified bodies of the Apis Bulls were buried.

**THE VALLEY OF THE KINGS**
Archeologists have uncovered more than 80 tombs in the Valley of the Kings, many of which you can visit. Unfortunately, most of the mummies are long gone. Some were removed by tomb robbers and others have ended up in museums. Today, Tutankhamun's mummy is the only one still lying in its tomb.

*Publicity poster for a recent movie featuring mummies*

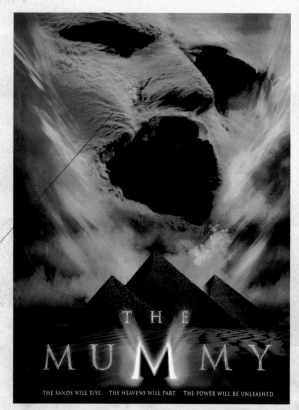

**THE EGYPTIAN MUSEUM**
In the Royal Mummy Room of the Egyptian Museum in Cairo, you can see the mummies of Ramses II, Seti I, and many other famous pharaohs. The museum also houses a collection of animal mummies, such as this ram.

Mummy case for a mummified ram

**MOVIES AND TELEVISION DOCUMENTARIES**
One of the best ways to keep up-to-date with the world of mummies is to look out for documentaries on television. These often feature the latest archeological finds, and you may well be able to watch a mummy being scanned or even unwrapped. You may also enjoy movies featuring mummies, but beware—these are not always strictly historically accurate!

Many of the valley tombs are beautifully decorated with wall paintings, like this scene from the tomb of Seti I

Cartouche

### HIEROGLYPHICS

Many ancient Egyptian mummy cases are covered with inscriptions. Hieroglyphics are difficult to learn to read, but one thing you can look out for is an oval shape, called a cartouche. This was only used to surround the hieroglyphs making up a pharaoh's name. So if you see a cartouche, it tells you that the mummy was a pharaoh.

These hieroglyphs appear on an obelisk at Luxor

### VISITING A MUSEUM

Some museums with the most extensive collections are shown in the box on the right, but many other museums around the world also contain mummies. In addition to the mummies themselves, museums often display information about X-rays and CT scans performed on their mummies, and what objects may be hidden inside the mummies' wrappings.

### USEFUL WEBSITES

Ancient Egypt site run by the British Museum:
**www.ancientegypt.co.uk**

Mummies and how they were made:
**www.si.edu/Encyclopedia_SI/nmnh/mummies.htm**

Maps and plans of tombs in the Valley of the Kings:
**www.friesian.com/tombs.htm**

Ötzi the Iceman and where he can be seen:
**www.bolzano.net/english/iceman-archaeological-museum.html**

The Roxie Walker Gallery at the British Museum in London

# Places to Visit

**MUSEUM OF FINE ART, BOSTON, MASSACHUSETTS**
The museum's exhibits allow visitors to examine burial customs from ancient Egypt to Roman times thorugh:
• finely painted sarcophagi and canopic jars
• a wide range of human and animal mummies.

**BRITISH MUSEUM, LONDON, ENGLAND**
This museum has the largest and most comprehensive collection of ancient Egyptian artifacts outside Cairo. Its exhibits include:
• impressive display of mummies and coffins
• body of Lindow Man, found preserved in a peat bog in Cheshire.

**EGYPTIAN MUSEUM, CAIRO, EGYPT**
A spectacular display of art and artifacts from ancient Egypt:
• Royal Mummy Room contains the mummies of Tuthmosis II, Seti I, Ramses II, and other legendary pharaohs
• museum also houses the Tutankhamun collection—around 1,700 treasures from the boy-king's tomb.

**MUMMIFICATION MUSEUM, LUXOR, EGYPT**
Displays explain the ancient Egyptian process of mummification and include:
• mummy and coffin of Maseharti, a high priest and general from the 21st dynasty period
• embalming equipment, such as instruments for removing internal organs and items needed by the mummy on its journey to the afterlife
• collection of mummified cats and rams.

**ROEMER- UND-PELIZAEUS MUSEUM, HILDESHEIM, GERMANY**
One of the premier Egyptian collections in the world. Exhibits include:
• Egyptian mummies, masks, and coffins
• mummies of cats, ibises, and a 12-ft (3.5-m) long crocodile
• collection of mummy bundles and other artifacts from Peru.

Death mask from a Chimu mummy bundle

# Glossary

**AFTERLIFE** Life after death.

**AMULET** A charm that the ancient Egyptians believed had magical powers to protect the body from evil or to bring good luck. Amulets often took the form of plants, animals, or parts of the human body.

**APIS BULL** A sacred bull, which the ancient Egyptian believed was an incarnation of the god Ptah. When the Apis Bull died, its body was mummified and buried in a special tomb called the Serapeum.

**ARCHEOLOGIST** A person who studies human history by excavating ancient sites and analyzing the buildings and remains found there.

**ARSENIC** Short for "arsenic trioxide," a white powdery substance that is highly poisonous.

**ATEF CROWN** A crown topped with two large feathers, which was one of the symbols of the Egyptian god Osiris.

**AUTOPSY** A scientific examination of a dead body, often to find out how the person died.

**BA** In ancient Egypt, one form of a dead person's spirit, often pictured as a bird with a human head.

**BACTERIA** Tiny microorganisms that cause some diseases and make dead bodies decay.

**BOG** A stretch of wet, spongy ground. Dead bodies can be naturally mummified in some types of bog, because bogs contain little oxygen and this stops the growth of bacteria that normally decay bodies.

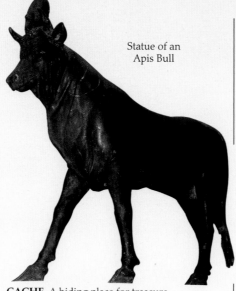

Statue of an Apis Bull

A model of DNA

**BOOK OF THE DEAD** In ancient Egypt, a collection of magic spells that was painted inside coffins or on a roll of papyrus left in a tomb. These spells were intended to help the dead person on their perilous journey to the next world.

**BOTANIST** A scientist who studies plants.

**CACHE** A hiding place for treasure. In Egyptology, the word is used to describe the secret hiding places where some royal mummies were concealed after their tombs in the Valley of the Kings had been looted by robbers.

**CANOPIC JAR** A jar with a lid in the shape of a god's head. Canopic jars were used to store the embalmed internal organs from an Egyptian mummy.

**CARTONNAGE** A material similar to papier mâché, made from scraps of linen or papyrus, gummed together with plaster or resin. In ancient Egypt, cartonnage was sometimes used to make mummy cases and mummy masks.

**CARTOUCHE** In ancient Egyptian writing, an oval shape containing the hieroglyphs that spelled out a pharaoh's name.

**CATACOMB** An underground cemetery, often in the form of a series of tunnels with recesses used as tombs.

**CT SCAN** A scan, similar to an X-ray, but which produces a three-dimensional (3-D) image of an object. A CT scans (also known as CAT scan) is short for "computerized axial tomography."

**DJED PILLAR** An amulet in the shape of a pillar. It was the symbol of the Egyptian god Osiris and represented survival, stability, and the possibility of life after death.

**DNA** Short for "deoxyribonucleic acid," a material which is present in all living organisms and carries their genetic information.

A djed pillar

**DYNASTY** A succession, or family, of kings who are related to each other. Historians divide the long list of Egyptian pharaohs into 30 dynasties.

**EMBALMING** A chemical process used to preserve a dead body and stop it from decaying.

**EXPOSURE** Death caused by being exposed to severe weather conditions, such as extreme wind and cold.

**FAIENCE** A form of decorated and glazed pottery (usually called Egyptian faience).

**FORENSICS** The application of biochemical and other scientific techniques to the investigation of crime. Forensic experts sometimes examine mummies to find out how they died.

**FREEZE-DRIED** Dried out by very cold weather conditions.

**GIRDLE OF ISIS** An amulet in the shape of a knot of cloth. It was the symbol of the Egyptian goddess Isis and represented her protective powers.

**GLACIER** A river of ice, which is slowly moving forward or retreating.

**GULLY** A ravine or channel that has been worn away by water.

**HIEROGLYPHICS** The form of writing used by the ancient Egyptians, in which pictures were used to represent words, syllables, or sounds.

**KA** In ancient Egypt, one form of a person's spirit.

**KOHL** A type of eye makeup used by the ancient Egyptians. Kohl was a black powder used to outline the eyes, similar to modern eyeliner.

**LATE PERIOD** The period of ancient Egyptian history that lasted from approximately 747 to 332 BCE.

**MIDDLE KINGDOM** The period of ancient Egyptian history which lasted from approximately 2055 to 1650 BCE.

**MUMMIFORM** In the shape of a mummy. The word is often used to describe the curved mummy-shaped coffins in which some Egyptians were buried.

A glacier

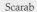

Scarab

**MUMMY CASE** A form of coffin, often made of wood or cartonnage, used to contain a mummified body.

**MUMMY MASK** A mask representing the face of the dead person that was placed over a mummy's face.

**NATRON** A naturally occurring form of salt found in dried lake beds. The Egyptians used natron to dry out a dead body before it was mummified.

**NEMES HEADDRESS** A distinctive, striped headdress of cloth folded over the hair, worn only by the Egyptian pharaoh.

**NEW KINGDOM** The period of ancient Egyptian history that lasted from approximately 1550 to 1069 BCE.

**NOMADS** People who have no settled home, but who wander from place to place in search of fresh pasture for their animals.

**OLD KINGDOM** The period of ancient Egyptian history that lasted from approximately 2686 to 2181 BCE.

**PAPYRUS** A material for writing on, used by the ancient Egyptians. It was made from strips of reed woven together and beaten to form long rolls like paper.

**PEAT** A brown deposit, similar to soil, formed from partly decomposed plants. Peat can be burned as a fuel.

**PECTORAL** An ornament or piece of jewelry that is worn on the chest. A pectoral was sometimes enclosed in an Egyptian mummy's bandages.

**PHARAOH** The ruler of ancient Egypt. The Egyptians believed that the pharaoh was a living incarnation of the god Horus, so he was treated with great respect.

**QUIVER** A bag in which an archer stored his spare arrows.

**RADIOCARBON DATING** A technique for finding the age of an organic object by measuring the amount of carbon-14 it contains. It can be used to date things like dead bodies or ancient plant remains.

**RADIOGRAPHER** A person who takes X-ray pictures, or operates a scanner.

**RISHI** Decorated with a feather design. The word comes from the Arabic word for "feathered."

**SAND BURIAL** An early form of burial used in ancient Egypt, in which the dead body was buried in the desert sand. The dry sand stopped the process of decay, and mummified the body naturally by drying it out.

**SARCOPHAGUS** A coffin made of stone. In ancient Egypt a sarcophagus was usually a stone box, into which the mummy in its coffin was placed. The name means "flesh eater" in Greek.

**SCARAB** An Egyptian amulet in the shape of a beetle.

**SHABTI** A small model figure of a servant or worker. The ancient Egyptians believed that in the afterlife they might be required to do hard manual work. Wealthy people were buried with shabti figures, who they believed would come to life and do this work for them.

**SHRINE** A casket or box containing sacred relics. In Egyptology, the word is used to describe one of a nest of boxes in which a pharaoh's coffin was placed.

**SHROUD** A large sheet of material used to wrap a dead body.

**TANNING** A process normally used to turn animal hides into leather by soaking them in a liquid containing tannic acid. Some bog mummies have also been tanned to preserve them.

**VALLEY OF THE KINGS** A secluded valley across the Nile from the town of Thebes (Luxor), where many Egyptian pharaohs were buried in hidden tombs.

An Egyptian document, written on papyrus

Wedjat eye

**VITAL ORGANS** Organs, such as the heart and brain, that are essential for keeping the body alive.

**WEDJAT EYE** An eye symbol believed to protect a mummy's health and give the body new vitality. It represented the eye of the god Horus, which was miraculously restored after he lost it in a fight with evil.

**XERORADIOGRAPH** A form of X-ray image that emphasises edges so that the outlines of shapes are easier to see.

# Index

# Acknowledgments

**Dorling Kindersley would like to thank:**
The staff of the Dept of Ancient Egypt & Sudan, British Museum, London, in particular Dr John H Taylor; Ian Mackay at the Museum of Mankind, London; Angela Thomas & Arthur Boulton of the Bolton Museum; John Saunders, Stephen Hughes, & the staff of the Dept of Medical Physics, St. Thomas' Hospital, London (p. 51); Reg Davis; Don Brothwell; Joyce Filer; Guita Elmenteuse; George Bankes at the University of Manchester; Theya Molleson at the Natural History Museum, London; the Seventh Earl of Carnarvon; the Egypt Exploration Society; Nicholas Reeves; William & Miranda MacQuitty; Peter Nahun; Maria Demosthenous; Martin Davies; Mitsuko Miyazaki; Martin Atcherley; Michael Dunning & Geoff Brightling for photography; Carole Andrews; Gillie Newman for illustrations on pp. 10 & 15; James Putnam for the illustration on p. 25; Belinda Rasmussen; Helena Spiteri, Sharon Spencer & Manisha Patel for design & editorial; Céline Carez for research.

**For this edition, the publisher would also like to thank:** Lisa Stock for editorial assistance, David Ekholm-JAlbum, Sunita Gahir, Susan Malyan, Susan St Louis, & Bulent Yusuf for the clip art; Sue Nicholson & Edward Kinsey for the wall chart; Monica Byles & Stewart Wild for proofreading; Margaret Parrish for Americanization.

**Picture credits:** a=above, b=below, c=center, f-far, l=left, r=right
**Ancient Art and Architecture Collection:** 56cr; **Ancient Egypt Picture Library:** 68bl; **Ardea, London Ltd:** 23ac; /**Akelindau:** 13br; /**John Mason:** 44bc; /**Peter Steyn:** 45ar; **Owen Beattie /University of Alberta:** 9br; **Birmingham Museum:** 64tl; **British Museum:** 23al, 28al, 29ar, 29br, 31ac, 34ar, 44ar, 59al, 59ar, 62bl, 64bl, 69bl, 71 bl, 71br; /**Robert Harding Picture Library:** 11br; **Jean-Loup Charmet:** 36al; **Chief Constable of Cheshire:** 58al; **Christopher Cormack/Impact:** 60al, 60ar, 60c, 60b, 61l, 61ar, 61cr, 61br; **Corbis:** 67tl, 67bl, 68cl; **Reg Davis:** 49al, 50al; **C. M. Dixon:** 63c; **Alistair Duncan:** 64tr; **Egyptian National Museum, Cairo / Giraudon /Bridgeman Art Library, London:** 38cl; **Egypt Tourist Office:** 15bc; **Electa, Milan:** 6cr; **E. T. archive:** 29al; **Mary Evans Picture Library:** 14ar, 17br, 29bcl, 36bl, 39c, 40al, 41cl; **Forhistorisk Museum, Moesgard:** 58b; **Ronald Grant Archive:** 40bc; **Griffith Institute, Ashmolean Museum, Oxford:** 24al, 35cb, 38br; **Hammer Film Productions/Advertising Archives:** 41al; **Robert Harding Picture Library:** 11al, 29acl, 38bl, 38c, 38ar, 39al, 39ar, 39br, 55al, 63ar; **Michael Holford:** 7cr, 29ac, 55ar; **Hulton-Deutsch Collection:** 16bl, 26br, 47cr; **Louvre, Paris/Bridgeman Art Library, London:** 11cr, 42al, /**Giraudon/Bridgeman Art Library, London:** 13ar, /**Photo R.M.N:** 10cl, 25al, 42bl; **MacQuitty Collection:** 7cr, 10ar; **Manchester Museum, University of Manchester:** 48b, 70br; **Mansell Collection:** 6ar, 10bl; **Musée de l'Homme, Paris:** 54br; **Museum of London:** 9bl; **National Museum, Copenhagen:** 58ar; **National Museum, Greenland:** 7c, 62-63b; **Oldham Art Gallery,** **Lancs/Bridgeman Art Library, London:** 43bc; ™ & © Lucasfilm Ltd. (LFL) 1981. All rights reserved. **Courtesy of Lucasfilm Ltd./BFI Stills:** 41tr; **Pelizaeus-Museum, Hildesheim:** 10tc, 12br, 14b; **Popperfoto:** 55c; 67cr; **Rex Features Ltd:** 6cl, 56bl, 56c, 57ar, 63acl; **Photo R.M.N.:** 27c; **Science Photo Library:** David Nunuk 66bl; **Silkeborg Museum, Denmark:** 9cl; **Sygma:** 36br, 38al, 50ar, 51bl, 56al, 57al, 56-57b; **University College, London:** 62ar; **Collection Viollet:** 11ar; **Werner Forman Archive:** /**Dallas Museum of Art, USA:** 69br; /**The Greenland Museum:** 66br; **Xinhua News Agency:** 63ac.

**Wall chart:** Owen Beattie: University of Alberta br (ice mummy); Corbis: Reuters fbr; DK Images: Bolton Metro Museum bl (mummy bundle); British Museum cra (boat), crb, tl; Egyptian Museum, Cairo tr; Michael Holford: c (mummy case).

**Jacket:** Front: Sandro Vannini/Corbis, b; British Museum, London, l. Back: Musée De L'homme, Paris, l.

All other images © Dorling Kindersley
For further information see: **www.dkimages.com**